The City Visible:
Chicago Poetry for the New Century

William J. Allegrezza and Raymond L. Bianchi, editors

Cracked Slab Books
Chicago   2007

ISBN 0-9786440-1-8
ISBN 13 978-0-9786440-1-7

Library of Congress Control Number: 2007902422

First Edition

Cover Drawing, *Oculus*, by Waltraud Haas.

Cracked Slab Books
PO Box 378608
Chicago, IL 60637

http://www.crackedslabbooks.com

Table of Contents

Introduction

When we began to put together the anthology which became *The City Visible: Chicago Poetry for the New Century*, we started with a premise of a poetic conversation that began in the late 1990's and has lasted until today among certain groups of poets in Chicago, Milwaukee, Madison, and a few other places.

The dialogue is between these poets who more or less care about the same things and whose work has influenced each others' like a series of Venn diagrams touching all and influencing some. There are many more poets and movements in Chicago which did not make this volume. There is a complete lack of Slam Poets and regional writers; these groups are strong in Chicago, and they have a press infrastructure that supports their work. In this volume you have a variety of poets writing on the edge— experimental, multilingual, internationally infused writing at the heart of the United States.

Chicago has always been a locus of communication. From its founding, it was Chicago's location as a city linking South, East, and West that made the city what it is, the hub of America. All one has to do is drive from north to south in Chicago to realize this since you cross the 25 railway lines that traverse the city.

Chicago has also been a place that many times has in spite of all its innovation been ignored by the poetic lights in New York and San Francisco. It is interesting, however, what has happened here over the past six years. Chicago has seen an explosion of reading series (Discrete, Series A, Danny's, Chicago Poetry Project, Powell's, Art Institute), small presses (Cracked Slab Books, Flood Editions, Beard of Bees, Answer Tag), magazines (*Conundrum, Antennae, Moria*), websites and blogs (Chicagopostmodern poetry.com, Samizdat, Golden Rule Jones).

Chicago will never be New York or San Francisco; it will always be a place of innovation but American innovation. So we present Chicago and its region's poetry to the world in this anthology. The work speaks for itself, and we feel that our city and our region will show the future of poetry in the United States. Chicago is always recreating itself. All one has to do is remember that the city burned in 1871, and it remade itself as the City Visible and a city set apart.

Raymond Bianchi

Foreword

The innovative anthology of my twenties was *15 Chicago Poets* (Chicago: The Yellow Press, 1976). Among its senior figures were Ted Berrigan and Alice Notley (Northeastern Illinois University and The Body Politic reading series on Lincoln Avenue); Gwendolyn Brooks, Haki Madhubuti, and Angela Jackson (Chicago State University and the Nommo Workshop), and Paul Carroll (University of Illinois Chicago), who headed three distinct poetics, all considered to be of the "outside." Of the bohemian wing of the New York School, Ted and Alice radiated authenticity and the absolute conviction that language was a major medium. A brilliant poet of unique voice and formal inventiveness, Gwendolyn Brooks was the city's Major Poet and winner of the Pulitzer Prize. Paul Carroll had edited a major literary magazine, *Big Table*, important in advancing New York School, Beat, and Black Mountain poetics, and single-handedly created the city's first creative writing program and its major reading series, The Poetry Center.

Other important influences were present in Chicago but not represented in the Yellow Press anthology. Michael Anania, an energetic poet, teacher, and poetry editor for Swallow Books, represented Pound-Olson poetics; Lisel Mueller, who was to win the National Book Award and Pulitzer Prize, was highly successful as a free-verse lyric poet; and John Frederick Nims, who had edited *Poetry*, was the city's leading traditional formalist.

Except for the ongoing Slam phenomenon and six years in the 70s when the Body Politic series brought lots of poets from New York and San Francisco, there was no sense of a poetry boom. No one moved to Chicago to take sustenance from the innovative poetry scene, and many young Chicagoans left for the East in search of what they imagined to be greater energy there. Robert Bly, who lived in a three stop-sign town in Minnesota, once described Chicago as "a fly-over city." As poets, teachers, Poetry Center board members, and editors of *New American Writing*, Maxine Chernoff and I knew we had to look Outward, which meant bringing the rest of the poetry world to Chicago.

This was to change in the 1990s, with the development of additional graduate writing programs at Chicago State University, School of the Art Institute, and Columbia College Chicago; the emergence of *Chicago Review* as a presence under the editorship of

9

Devin Johnston and others to follow; related phenomena such as the arrival of Andrew Zawacki and Peter and Michael O'Leary at University of Chicago; the reading series I curated at Columbia College, which featured poets such as Charles Bernstein, Barbara Guest, Nathaniel Mackey, Cole Swensen, Michael Palmer, Jorie Graham, Brenda Hillman and Robert Hass, Ann Lauterbach, Gustaf Sobin, and Harryette Mullen; and the emergence of numerous independent reading series like the Danny's Tavern and Discrete series, founded by Columbia College students Greg Purcell and Kerri Sonnenberg; John Tipton's series at the Harold Washington Library; and the Myopic Series.

It was not until roughly 2000 that Chicago opened to postmodern strategies in poetry. In 1999, University of Chicago Press became Charles Bernstein's publisher and has remained so. That innovative writers Robyn Schiff and John Keene are considered acceptable to teach in the English Department at Northwestern University is a sign of aesthetic change not only for Chicago, but also literary culture as a whole. This is the kind of writing represented in *The City Visible*. It has intelligence, complexity, wit, emotional texture, and a variety of alternative formal strategies, as can be seen, for example, in Jesse Seldess' "In Contact," which creates a haunting minimalist lyric by circulating and subtly altering the words of an abbreviated lexicon: "Hand talking / Close up / By past will / Hand talking by / Tend / With incompletely / Finding view / And talking by / To be / And Walking by / Close up." Or consider Ed Roberson's Chicago evening lakescape, "Sight Read of a Couple of Stars," with its gorgeous attention to the poetic line: ". . . the world suite we play in on / time, or our missed cue, wherever / we come in, our / origin we don't understand making / as to achieve creation on / arrival . . ." It's tempting for me to refer to this postmodern, new millennial poetry as "The New Modernism," as I did in an essay of that title:

> At the turn of the century, consciousness is increasingly multiple. This is partly due to our changing models of communication, from the singular to the plural, from three networks to eighty-four channels. But representation has always been "double," like the shadows in Plato's cave. It involves the thing-as-thing and thing-as-language, an author in negotiation with a reader, and the many complexities of identity and difference. Poetry reflecting

that doubleness (cf. Stevens and Ashbery) is more realistic because it acknowledges the impact of the writing act on the resulting text. The truest poetry is reflexive, or self-mirroring. Paradoxically, without the presence of the world, the mind's reflection on its own devices is a useless solipsism.[1]

What we call innovative in poetry is a portrait in language of the world *as is* and therefore, *as possible*; it is a form of realism. Far from the false diegesis, or truth-seeming, of film fantasy, this kind of realism can be difficult for the U. S. reader to comprehend. He and she often seek fables and moral imaginaries that come already packaged: "My Father, in Heaven, Is Reading Out Loud." What we need is the greater experience of language as world-making—a language craft crash landing in fields of being = accuracy = art. Not recitations of the known but "tuning what the sky slips on over itself" (Kristy Odelius).

The title of this collection is well-chosen. Chicago has always been visible, even to the fly-over population. It is now more visible in language.

Paul Hoover

---

[1] *Fables of Representation: Essays.* Ann Arbor: University of Michigan Press, 139.

Srikanth Reddy

Bio: Srikanth Reddy's first collection of poetry, *Facts for Visitors*, received the Asian American Literary Award for Poetry in 2005. His poetry has been published in numerous journals, including *APR, Fence, Grandstreet, jubilat*, and *Volt*. A graduate of the Iowa Writers' Workshop and doctoral candidate at Harvard University, Reddy is currently an Assistant Professor of English at the University of Chicago.

Poetic Statement:

I'm interested in what might be thought of as the ethical dimension in poetic writing. For a long time it seems to me that poets have deliberately fled the ethical aspect of the art, in favor of (very important) explorations of the natural world, identity, representation, or any number of other areas. And of course, one could argue that a literary engagement in each of these areas leads in turn toward a more refined and aware "ethical" stance in the world. (The view that writing about nature makes one a better person, for example, makes a lot of sense to me). But I think—and this may be because, from the beginning, I've been faced with the question of writing about "postcolonial" experience—that poetry might offer ways of thinking about duty and injustice and obligation that other forms of writing (even ethical philosophy) can't open up. This has to do, I think, with the fact that our ethical nature is rooted in our linguistic nature, and that experiments in language can make available new ways of thinking about how to treat one another. Or, and this is pretty much the same thing, these experiments in language can make "old" ways of thinking about how to treat one another "new" all over again.

Corruption

I am about to recite a psalm that I know. Before I begin, my expectation extends over the entire psalm. Once I have begun, the words I have said remove themselves from expectation & are now held in memory while those yet to be said remain in expectation. The present is a word for only those words which I am now saying. As I speak, the present moves across the length of the psalm, which I mark for you with my finger in the psalm book. The psalm is written in India ink, the oldest ink known to mankind. Every ink is made up of a color & a vehicle. With India ink, the color is carbon & the vehicle, water. Life on our planet is also composed of carbon & water. In the history of ink, which is rapidly coming to an end, the ancient world turns from the use of India ink to adopt sepia. Sepia is made from the octopus, the squid & the cuttlefish. One curious property of the cuttlefish is that, once dead, its body begins to glow. This mild phosphorescence reaches its greatest intensity a few days after death, then ebbs away as the body decays. You can read by this light.

Everything

She was watching the solar eclipse
through a piece of broken bottle

when he left home.
He found a blue kite in the forest

on the day she lay down
with a sailor. When his name changed,

she stitched a cloud to a quilt
made of rags. They did not meet,

so they could never be parted.
So she finished her prayer,

& he folded his map of the sea.

14

Jennifer Scappettone

photo credit: Juliana Spahr

Bio: Jennifer Scappettone lived on both US coasts and in Italy and Japan before moving to Chicago. In Japan she created the cross-arts journal *MonZen;* in the Bay Area she co-curated the 21st-Century Poetics and the Holloway Poetry Series. Her works include *From Dame Quickly* (poems), *Abluvion Almanac* (a chapbook of graphic stills), *Locomotrix: Selected Poetry of Amelia Rosselli* (translations from the Italian), *Venice and the Digressive Invention of the Modern* (a study of the obsolescent topos as a crucible for modernism), and *Exit 43* (an archaeology of the landfill and opera of pop-ups in progress, commissioned by Atelos Press). She works as an Assistant Professor at the University of Chicago.

Poetic Statement: Manifest

The relationship of the lyric to public life. The relationship of poetic structures to historical structures. The relationship, and possible complicity, of poetic torquing to discursive manipulations at large.

Whether or not a personal poet can engender a collective expression. Whether there is or may be a lyric we that doesn't hum battle hymns of the republic or worse.

Who is speaking. When one is speaking now how many generations of speakers are speaking through one, even as one considers oneself a broad-spectrum auto-arbiter. How many arguments are teeming within any single word.

Which forces make experience coherent or communicable— love, damage—and which of these scream for what has been named lyric expression in this historical moment. Hence the relationship of this particular moment to other particular moments. Historical empathy.

Which forces expose the schisms of that experience in critical ways.

How the poem resists the alienation of sensuous experience from humans. How it participates in the alienation of sensuous

15

experience from humans. How it might resist its die-hard
recruitment by forces of commodification. How it differs or doesn't
from Dame Quickly: is it fish, flesh, or a spectral thing that speaks
back?

The square and the box as oppositional structures: outing
versus cloistering—public versus oikonomic—talk. The word
trafficking between these zones, as trafficking invokes an exchange
of the feminine—as the feminine is mapped onto the body, the
archaic, the aesthetic at once.

How the poem gives body to the waste of time. How the
poem gives body to the discarded or the undisposed. With a
vengeance.

Derrida Is Dead 2.009

Gestation—Monstrosity—Blessed Event, a bulbous token of Saxon
craftsmanship that was a peripheral girlhood fame: precocious capacity
to recite all the Goebel catalog names. Minor cut from there
    into antiquarian
exile, the kind that makes you beat with the locals about the acanthus
    until your evening
spaghettum is theirs. Later I sat at the edge of another stairwell under
    Kent, extracting dowels
that passed for bones thrown down to you, recurrent chessmaster.
    Nightmare matology's
morning now. World was in defaced. That was a line from Rilke before
    the Thurn und Taxis
got to him, us. Dee Dee of Foxboro, you were my only love, once, before
    I knew only—what it was—
& Merr Angelina sold the landless shack to the son for a buck to taxi.
The non-sight of a pottery roof would import some dawn feeling, the
    sort impressing that village
hasn't yet been mistressed to administered air. That is, the lacunas
    haven't yet been curred
of their abashing stains on Stein's mattress. Or moss activating in the

16

kept address of
bedarling's gams already always. Guy fainted after Paul and Frances
queasy revolsed
hemselves; he must have been downing those empathies before the
fax, or at blathering cure would have trained those rimes out of
abluvion. That was a line divided and Burgundy cast out over the
fosse.

da s

I was pre-Pandoran once, clear & amok, scarlet free where scarcely
orange or purple romed: all
font, Greek, drunk, then, then Tyred, vinegar aspect for breakfast. How I
seam now in video
footage of national folding where only arson lives lives. Its source is
valid because Google
calls it 100% relevant and government, which is apt since it's an
historical event. I reseek and
pall this chunk's vocation. Viatical my neighbor asks if I'd ride
in the trunk, no kid; my
hatchback is mined in the parking lot for its sparkplugs beyond the
bar. She masking
he then is captured by the faith-based; once she creams, he stops calling
it
vocation. Down here, they have imported the clouds from Japan, & I
hear them, sardine.
Keez me, gaghrl, yr old won. Geta-crushing Shoji of the air
will remember cat-noise
and -fish for complements as the King of Terror will never have forced
the possible Fed you you you're not—not. Postal will be yours and you,
bulk predellal, tardy
urinals on vehicles, art naught but an empty he-port. Grey they err over
joy, toupeeing space
as picture meant to do. I stream, hand mover, reek, occupy ice and call

17

that night. Of all indecipherably
you finally type to say you hosted Uncle Chen in your backyard
exclusive. Wake, it's time to smell the smoke. Darling I

incensed. One could have been your she-port; pretty noun
look ahead to repast and yr Gruyerer aspect. Hype alone remains inside
the box.

Suzanne Buffam

Bio: Suzanne Buffam grew up in Canada and moved to the States to attend the Iowa Writers' Workshop. She is the author of *Past Imperfect*, a collection of poems published in 2005 with House of Anansi Press, and *Interiors*, a chapbook published in 2006 with Delirium Press in Montreal.

Her poems have appeared in numerous journals in Canada and the U.S., including *The Denver Quarterly*, *Poetry*, *The Canary*, *Jubilat*, and *A Public Space*. She now lives in Chicago and teaches creative writing at the University of Chicago.

Poetic Statement:

I like the part in the *Poetics* where Aristotle explains how the best Tragic effects depend on the combination of the Inevitable and the Unexpected. I guess that's how I try to write: I want to surprise myself, without shirking a sense of consequence from one line or one sentence to the next. Sometimes I think I would like to write something long one day, because that seems to me truly heroic, but, on the other hand, Emerson's got a good point when he says "the meaner the type by which a law is expressed, the more pungent it is."

Anaktoria

after Sappho

The committee met on the first of the month to decide once and for all which of this black planet's myriad sights most honors the bold, high peaks of the human heart. A young man brought down his fist with a thud. There is nothing in this world, he cried, more stirring to the soul than a good parade! Sun striking the trumpets, the flash of batons, wind licking the flags into blazing bright sails . . . Just then a fleet of gold jets roared past the high windows in tight formation. Everyone looked up and gasped, stars in their eyes, and seemed on the point of consensus. A frail old man in a pale grey suit and matching cravat cleared his throat. Slow ripples moved through the room as he spoke, firmly, and not without eloquence, on behalf of the twin Spanish replica tall ships that had sailed that Spring into harbor, bringing sailors and replica guns, firing replica cannons into the salt-sweetened air each evening at nine o'clock sharp. Some smiled to themselves and looked at their hands, some gingerly closed their reports, leaned forwards in their seats and eyed the heavy wooden gavel in the chairman's hand. But I, who had been listening at the door for some time, distracted from my task (as happens often, and for which I am often sternly rebuked), slipped down the dim hall and out into the night where I joined the parade that had swallowed you.

Mariner

Sometimes I eat an orange and completely forget about dying. Nonetheless, the thought of home can reliably be said to bring tears to the eyes of any traveller. When the sailor travels inland, he misses not so much the sight of the ocean as the sound it makes beneath him at night when the world has disappeared and there are only stars above to guide him. Perhaps he also misses the smell of creosote in the breeze, but it remains so utterly abstract in its absence he cannot properly be said to *feel* the lack. On the other hand, I find it possible to miss what I have never known. My voice has been described as nondescript, yet I continue to use it. I call to the hills and to the good people in them. I call to hear the sound of my own voice. The truth is, I seldom think about home at all. To grow up at sea is a mixed blessing, granted, but show me a blessing that isn't.

Best Case Scenario

At second glance the leaves are bright green
and the dog is asleep. The omelette slides

from the pan intact. No one we know
serves us tea. It is sweet. It tastes faintly

exotic but also sad, like the jasmine blossoms
wilting in our hair. High, high above,

clouds grind light into dust-motes.
Because we have not died yet of hope,

nor its opposite, we remain here among
these creaturely feelings, indentured

to the small brown birds that will not
light on our hair. So be it. Our shadows

on the grass may be luckier, although
their fate is such that they won't know it.

John Tipton

Bio: John Tipton is the author of *surfaces* (Flood Editions, 2004). His translation of Sophocles' *Ajax* is forthcoming from Flood.

Poetic Statement:
I always try to make something beautiful.

Dear Markov,

I counted the words that you asked
set them in rows took their logarithms
but there spoils the proof the words
the method yields a remainder but one
(of which window did they fall out?)
message decays with time yet remain messages
if we can number them by hand
what did string on the finger forget?
but something sits just under the phonetics
perhaps a submarine beneath the polar cap
blind & voiceless it echoes the cold
noun trapped inside which will slowly suffocate
before its spellings collapse & it implodes
have we become those tragic sailors, Andrei?

-Shannon

Good Shannon,

I see the method has misled you
when I say *method* you hear *map*
it approximates English never really being so
think in terms of atomic models, Claude
while you scruple the surface it glares
sound & sense seduce with their friction
what broken phrase is not to hear?
you seem as if someone is reading
just like Whorf & his fictive Eskimo
the ad hoc nonsense names for snow
you counted the words but you failed
to go & speak with that Eskimo
bent over a hole in the ice
waiting for anything to rise & breathe

-Markov

syntax at Moab

that sky extends its bounds by nine
's not captured in the weather predicate

is it gypsum makes the desert shine?
this sun gives absence in discrete terms

it blocks the pathway of the said
wouldn't let [IP her [I ∅] [VP [V speak] each word]]

there discovers the thief of the infinitive
where dryness forms the grain of atmospheres

what did those words drift like ravens
as we repeat them seven years ago?

this question marks the place it departs
& begs movement of the spectacular clouds

it tried T. to hear transitive gestures
& the minimal not & bothers him

but everyone describes a picture of herself
imagines the slant rain a glance blurs

what jointed phrase we'll have, my dear
while our clauses crack in the afternoon

Utah severs to remember & drops apart
the tense that we use not saying

we cannot unlearn to think what portions
the choice of things bare & keen

Eric Elshtain

Photo Credit: Jon Trowbridge

Bio: Eric Elshtain's poetry, reviews, and interviews have appeared in such journals as *American Letters & Commentary, Chicago Review, Denver Quarterly, Kiosk, Literary Review, McSweeney's, New American Writing, Ploughshares, PomPom, Skald,* and others. Elshtain's latest chapbook, *Here in Premonition,* was published in 2006 by RubbaDucky Press (Brooklyn/Chicago). He edits Chicago's on-line Beard of Bees Press.

Poetic Statement:

The ear is my ruler—my queen and my measure—when I write poetry. Led by sound, words find functions that differ from description and denomination, from narrative and discursive sense. Messages broadcast from ear-to-ear, hopefully making the lips move before the mind kicks-in with its meaning governor.

Methods of Taphonomy
to Chris Tysh

iii.

You need phronesis
to lead the dance
& not miss the measure

while you're beneath
the everything-edge
you spent one night without

But I'm making this up
as you go along, aren't I?

ii.

Those novels always refer
to readers at some point
cheek to cheek

all the way no matter
what you call spaces.
You fell for dolls as a girl.

But you're making me up
as I go along, aren't you?

i.

"All I see is the flags"
but too dark to see what
colors fly before masts

& the mezuzah become symbols
in your 'scape that always ends
& hence gets meaning.

Aren't we upping this go
as we un-make along?

The *Message* is the Message

Christ, yes, my voodoo
organism crackles 3 ways fuels
that into formal glories turn.

Sin-dazzled aquamen span
an open ocean range sailors
take for waxworks of land

& gimcrackery cast out by He
who unseats sawdust Caesars.
For who slouches after our

social smoke, knocks up the skylark
but those hosts of lords?
& how safe is it to call sarx

a storm & not fire the closer
Truth gets to Her Mars
& its 8 angstroms of care?

Light will do our eyes
with the sex of Itself—
a half-tone skin-trick

looped into the pyx
fish- and loafless
until Athens fell: Christ-

fallen, yes; obeah-man's
Amen! Seizure's reason!
5 fates away from a new phylum!

Diode to René Daumal as a Teenager

An ether creep stirs
femto-seconds to re-

create Small Bangs

& made you chance
there cells of chandelier
limbs ten-candles lit

Over the craft sunk
to be dove to
six syllables deep

Your drift no novel
could refer twice to
mouthing home box-kites

Up numbered no-where
Buddha better than
Gamma ray flag-men

met... you her... my wish?

Lodestone
for Matthias

The kava-cup grit's bitter sends shivers as when my body stopped short spine first standing-to to the dead snake Bill asked me to toe off the road while driving Poudre Canyon towards Indian Meadows to arc Elk-hair Caddis into the air & onto the promise of a tense surface & there-about trout but ofttimes the flies go under with the weight of water—like kava makes mock of gravity but tends to a paradoxical flop of the somatic as the minded sphere goes caddis waft left & weft with conifer along the banks where somewhere someone sometime banked his battle & lowered a gun's satcheled powder into a rock-crease with some buckshot black like eyes of tiny bees dried in old comb swept up from the floor of the tornado shed & the kava says I haven't the sand for this kind of isobar—loosed across a hemisphere's immense music: "I know a few fucking things about this war situation," Matthias says three

April's ago "and none of them isn't completely fucked up." The kava boils & remembers how it recently spotted a blowfish impossibly sunk half into a sand crab lair, how it carried it on the sole of a sandal to the ocean's edge where dead a mind unfolded specialized scales impossible to swallow, except for a sky made gullet by planets—throated stones grinding out time & time again a gravitas that binds orb to orb for epic spins.

David Pavelich

Bio: David Pavelich lives in Chicago and works at the University of Chicago as a special collections librarian. He edits and publishes Answer Tag Home Press, a small press publishing chapbooks and broadsides in limited editions. His poems have appeared in *Antennae, Aufgabe, Bird Dog,* and other journals, and prose has appeared in *Chattahoochee Review* and *The Progressive Librarian.* Two chapbooks of his poems have been published: *Outlining* (Cuneiform Press) and *Ash* (Bronze Skull Press).

Poetic Statement:

Outside of my building in a sad planter are even sadder geraniums, shaking in wind; my window shade swings in the same breeze. "What may be incomplete as sculptural entities are of significance to the whole," wrote sculptor Isamu Noguchi in his definition of *garden.* His combination of abstraction with organic elements and his relief (finally) at the usefulness of art are instructive to me, too. Where I can't think of poems being read as "gardens" – as multidirectional, as lacking in sequence, approached from endless equal beginnings – I can think of them as wanting to be composed with that in mind. The line, the stanza (the shade, the geranium) as poetic entities might seem alone even in their immediate context, but should stand "to mean" at the close of the poem. And the poem – itself something in the shared wind – can defer its meaning until the end of the series. At any level, mine hopes to be a practice of feeling from objects, and lines made of objects of feeling, from the front door where those little pink flowers lose their leaves.

West

for Jesse Seldess

This could be the way
of the building back,

without size
the early line

pulled back to the copper
neighborhood.

Open a corner.
The world of air,

the children's field,
a wall of insulation

without size.
Lift up your distance –

this could be the way
of the building forward,

this could be a kind of
made wood.

Pursuant

In hand, who comes in to serve
the other. Or pond, or black river.
It was gone for the world they dissolved.

Then the silent stand. And recline away
from this, street to street to black river.
In the moth of the night

all wings become transparent.

Peter O'Leary

Bio: Born in Detroit, 1968. Raised in Grosse Pointe Park, a suburb of Detroit, educated in public schools there and then in a Catholic high school, De LaSalle Collegiate, taught by the LaSallean Christian Brothers. Post-secondary education at the University of Chicago, the College, earning an AB in English literature in 1990 and a PhD from the Divinity School in 1999. Epistolary contact with poet Ronald Johnson was initiated in 1992, followed by a few valuable meetings in San Francisco. Mentored by RJ until his death in 1998. Asked to be his literary executor. This charge has resulted in three books: *To Do As Adam Did: Selected Poems* (Talisman House, 2000);*The Shrubberies*, a collection of last poems (Flood Editions, 2001); & *Radi os* (Flood, 2005), a reprint. So far, two poetry books, *Watchfulness* (Spuyten Duyvil, 2001) and *Depth Theology* (Georgia, 2006) and one critical book, *Gnostic Contagion: Robert Duncan & the Poetry of Illness* (Wesleyan, 2002). Since 1986, have lived, on & off, in Chicago, with stints in Portland, Oregon, Detroit, Ann Arbor, Vienna, Budapest, & St. Louis. Since late 2001, residency in Berwyn, on the west side of Chicago, in a house, with wife & two sons.

Poetic Statement: THE DYNAMIC CORE

"It appears," muses neurobiologist Gerald M. Edelman, proposing a model of consciousness, "that the dynamic reentrant thalamocortical system" – which he elsewhere calls "the dynamic core" – "speaks mainly to itself." Through language, consciousness becomes increasingly, richly aware of itself. As sentience is to consciousness, so myth is to language. If language is a process of higher-order consciousness, then myth is its dynamic core – metaphor itself, the grand associative soul of our species.

Robert Duncan famously insisted that myth "is the story told of what cannot be told," adding, "[w]herever life is true to what mythologically we know life to be, it becomes full of awe, awe-full." The word is a *mysterium tremendens*; or, in a coinage, a *lutrescence* – something so intense with light you sense it rotting.

("A more profound sphere of things," Teilhard de Chardin called God.) Let's not leave theology to religion; let's liberate theology to talk about poetry, which is, above all, myth's sacred, therapeutic attendances. "But what I speak of here in terms of a theology," warns Duncan, "is a poetics." Which is a beginning.

To Epithymitikon
(the soul's desiring power)

Nodal pyrolatry, brume of gold, honey dusk.
Lightning tesserated, psychic pollen, encombed augur.
Roman foretime, abundant stasis, cenobitic dream.
Risen figures, ripened nectars, ultimate geometry.
Icon of thunderclaps,
icon of minute harvests.
Astromantic icons.
Nocturnal radiance, sulphured umber, knowledge of morning.
Slanted recess, multiplication of the Mother, folded cherubic pinions.
Gestures of blessing, lutrescent balm, serum of gold.
Angelic benison, incanted longings, flux of gold.
Encrypted rafters, storied arches, golden nebula.
Conic insufflation, oleagine of light.
Old Testament corridor, Biblical God.
Annunciated seed, archangelic lily.
Reanimation of antique devotions.
Reliquary of gloomiest monitions.
Unction of dazzle, Pentecostal spokes, pantrocratic awe.
Unguent of eyesight, afterimage of ordered throngs, evangelists' support.
Calligraphic compression, glare of judgment, stooping seraphs.
Himation's zinc, love of suffering, the Church within the Church.
Love of miracles.
Love of cupolas & marble.
Love of gold's concentration lengthened by vision into ash of brass.
Mantled altar, depth of the monstrance, paradisaic glass.
Crepuscular forecast, inverted tomb, cathedral of animate dread.
Glimmered imago, dove in emanation, incorporated, orbic sphericity.
Apiary of light harvests, nave of golden petition.
Spirit cataracts, infinite curvature of time.

Ebulliences

> Creation is God overboiled.
> SAINT BERNARD OF HYDE, *THE MYSTICAL HISTORIES*

THERE IT IS MORE INWARD THAN IT CAN BE TO ITSELF

God.
Autoluminescent, sourceless ember
that lights up the pearly-lambent jelly nebulae – holy *luce divina* –
whose expanding lantern like a fluke of lightning through bright heaven
fulminates. Shrines of plasmic candles the universe – lymphic – is. The
      light lies

Deep within your vision of it &
can't satisfy your demands. The darkness is
a Gothic noontide glare each cathedral enshadows epochally in
time & soul. A summit essence inverted, clear
as flame, expansively pitched from above.

Aglow. God is gone up.
The God of Abraham. *Let the daughters be glad*. The most
enlightened *facula*, a monocular Seraph – God-fixed –
feasts its intellective appetites not on fire
but on light. Comprehending the upper darkness not. Comprehending

Evening – its beamy desolations that *burneth the chariot in fire* –
not. Further down, an archangelic dunce fails to register shadow.
Leaving you in its jetted plumes. To peer into the hydrogen syrup
of our nethermost sun, alone. Its
light abyss. Transpicuous, rutilant, sunk.

Bassolith.
Of thrummed light. Bariolage
of darkness & of flame. Raiment. Of glad needlework.
Luteous fuel of sulphur; saffron beam of transplendency.
Bass tone. Of fulver. Atramentous grave note. Of his voice
death sounds from, slugged.

We cannot stand to hear God speak.

34

Phosphor. And flicker. And flash. And reflection.
And fulgor. And grave. And glory. And earth melted. And gladness.
And sepulcher. And shimmer. And luster. And ink. And citrus. And
resonance. And gift.
And flame. And flame & flame.

Our ears can bear the aftersound,
the enriched silence full of Him.

And the slurring of the lightnotes.
And the glorious Biber excesses of it.
And its madcap last-minute grandeurs.

And his inward thought is, A grand flame follows a tiny scintilla.
And the triumph of it should flume. And
it should flume. And it should
flume.

THAT HIS BREAKING THROUGH IS NOBLER THAN HIS FLOWING OUT

Come.
Receive the spirit of wisdom
& the spirit of holiness: the spirit
of glory thundered & the spirit of the fear
of God: the spirit of the light of knowledge &
the spirit of the descent of the soul into the bruising
temperatures of self-awareness: the spirit of the dew
of fire & the evil spoiler hidden in its glare.

Bless the weakly looking eye: bless the puzzling ass of scripture: bless
the great condescension of God: bless the fierce
Assyrian flame that prefigured
him: bless the deeps
afraid at his presence: bless the spiritual powers
that tremble before him: bless the sea
he has walled in sand: bless the heavens he has
stretched out like a curtain: bless the light
obedient to him

who makes the clouds his chariot:
who has desolated lives countlessly: who
speaks in the City & through the Land: who betrays lovingkindness
through the ignostic gestures
of worshipful men: who has hasted
away: who has roared, troublous: who has burgeoned inly
but irretrievably even to the most compassionating, the most watchful,
the most
caring: who hushes: who is latent as his constellation

at noonday, manifest in light's excess only: who looks
on the earth & it trembles: who breaks
the jaws of the land with oceanic fists:
who deserves my steadfast contemplation: who
mocks me from my bookshelves: *who coveredst the earth*
with the deeps

out of which, oneiromantic, three inventions
intersect—:

          in the backyard, in the wintry predawn, looking up into
the southern sky, a deep, resonant streak of cobalt blue & fathomless
as if made up of starry light. But this smear is
self-lambent. Pearly. And there's no way to peer all the way into its
depth. Its coherence. Its grumed thickness. So that
it seems epiphanic. In spite of the incredible cold. Or
a visitation. A resonator.

Two, in fact. Though the instrument is strange & sits
unused, I know how to play it. Tuned to fifths, the blubbering strings
stretch across two chambers, each
generating separate sounds harmonized
when the dozen strings are played – the instrument is whole, a
conjoined gamba. It's on a shelf. I
pull it out – admiring the tuning pegs made
from choirmasters' fingerbones.

At the window, nearby, in the light of her kitchen –
angelic? – the centenarian wearing
a white bonnet. She's reading.
The Bible.

The book's cloth is indigo'd.
Atmospheric. Royal. Cynanic.
Blue.

Θ Θ Θ

The surplus of valid signs makes meaning boil inferentially,
darkly over into the realm
of fantasy whose singular angle of
inclination disorients you
specifically enough
to call it your
idiom.

William Fuller

Bio: William Fuller grew up in Barrington, Illinois, received his Ph.D. in English from the University of Virginia (1983) and is the author of *The Coal Jealousies* (Coincidence, 1987), *byt* (O Books, 1989), *The Sugar Borders* (O Books, 1993), *Aether* (Gaz, 1998), *The Central Reader* (Paradigm Press, 1999), *Roll* (Equipage, 2000), *Three Poems* (Barque, 2000), *Avoid Activity* (Rubba Ducky, 2003), *Sadly* (Flood Editions, 2003), and *Watchword* (Flood Editions, 2006); *Dry Land* is forthcoming from Equipage. He lives in Winnetka, Illinois and works in the Trust Department of The Northern Trust Company, Chicago.

Poetic Statement:
    A false abstracte cometh from a fals concrete.

The lesion is word, wounding is the work.

In the Cave of Mirrors

Heraclitus the Stoic records Heraclitus the Obscure as saying: 'We step and do not step into the same rivers; we are and are not.' Thought steps and does not step into an entangling coolness. New water, intelligible as daylight, approaches and departs. Evanescence doctors stability, while the good Ephesians, gnomic and intermittent, pace in and out of time. Their anxiety is broadly allocated over these compressed views. They are and are not held in mirrors, inclined toward sleep. The walls of the cave comprise the silence outside, which accretes in the coils of the ear. In *The E at Delphi* Plutarch cites Heraclitus's teaching that 'all things are an equal exchange for fire, and fire for all things, as goods are for gold, and gold for goods.' The unchanging rhythms of exchange express the constant totality. What exhausts the circuit signifies its revival, without surplus or deficit. Gold is fire, the dialectical solvent, substratum and act: its vacant murmurings vest the appetites; crooked and straight, it kindles and extinguishes the mind. Shining above crude rivers the moon sickens with it. It steps and does not step, restlessly still.

The Sun Is Raining

Miles Champion once said that certain things relevant to prediction of behavior warrant discussion without reference to our existing theories. For the assumptions lurking in such theories can render one insensible. Resignation follows this insight in the form of a bright blue flash emerging from damp twigs. No one wants to capture a physical state that misleads. Nor is it appropriate to objectify its absence. 'Suddenly the seat flips up and I have a sensation of pain.' Somewhere, out there, the truth comes ashore. Roughly, we divide ourselves in two groups, the vicious and the mild. Time distills a single essence from both and walks it up the long staircase to twin rainy skies.

Mobile Steam Plant/Spare Change

If and only if the magic pig were a case of sincerity having been
eclipsed by deceit then feeding it abuses the practice whereby it is
eventually dispersed into those for whom no such questions arise.
Patient but distracted, joining smokestacks and steeples to points of
time distinguished by depth and sunk perpendicular to the landing
strip, you direct them in writing to restore the site before the snow
returns, electing not to be controversial by consenting to violate
abandoned policy—
            written in birdseed
      your eyes are cold
improvident
lover hastily calls
precious, precious
it was jealousy—
but hard hints like yours
        make a man avoid the earth
           I quote

Michael O'Leary

Bio: Michael O'Leary is the co-founding editor of *LVNG* magazine and the co-founding editor of Flood Editions. He is currently pursuing a Ph.D. in materials engineering at the University of Illinois at Chicago.

Poetic Statement:

Poetry is an atlas to the world of language, its longitude consciousness, its latitude music.

King of Babylon

*There and then the sentence was carried out upon
Nebuchadnezzar.*
                              Daniel 4:30

When the king of Babylon came
to the U.S.A.
he was dreaming of two rivers
where his gardens sway.

He followed all the waters down
to Little Egypt
where the Ohio and the Mississippi
meet up.

Waiting for his satraps
and magicians to gather,
the king ran into a kid
looking for his father

who held a praying mantis
in the palm of his hand.
When evening came with a gentle
breeze across the land

and blew through a willow stand,
King Nebuchadnezzar
coolly stroked his saffron beard
and shook his eagle feathers:

"How the black hammer of the earth
is cut asunder.
How the cities have been abandoned
to plunder.

When I heard them say to the mountains,
'Please, fall on us,'
I sought, like pharaohs before me,
the wisdom of Memphis

in the twitch of sheep's guts.
How was I supposed to know
who Jeremiah was
or where my gods would go?"

The kid listened beneath a willow
and handed him his wine
made of rotten crabapples floating
in turpentine.

Oh! be joyful, it's a wicked
life now isn't it?
The wind blows but no one knows
when or where it visits.

Who's right and who's written?
A wicked life now isn't it?
The wind speaks but no one seeks
wisdom from a prophet.

The king of Babylon sashayed
backward gazing west
when the kid brandished an ax
and commenced to bless

the willow tree with a swift stroke
straight through its pith
leaving only a stump
and a bug to dance with.

King Nebuchadnezzar paused
to watch the lovely crown
of his willow twist through
the confluence, sinking down:

"Bury me on the warm waters
of the Euphrates.
Float my bloated body down
the Mississippi,

past Cyrus, past Xerxes,

past Alexander,
past the pigs at Shiloh,
past Anaximander.

Bury me in the waters
of the Mississippi,
float my body down to the tune
of Old Dixie

past all the moon-eyed ladies
and schools of gibbous fish
where there's no noon
and the only wisdom's indifference."

The kid stood up and turning
in every direction
watched cities like fireflies
light a broken procession.

Oh! be joyful there's no hope
in abomination.
Love of what has been spoken
is renunciation.

Oh! be joyful what the wind says
nobody can tell.
In the absence of war you must make
war on yourself.

The Chills

The street quite still.
Down the long corridor

a light, several doors
and a single pine.

Conversation on
the wires are quiet,

sequestered from here
to there, ear to ear.

The most intimate
jokes get lost sometimes,

even simple questions
go unanswered.

Quiet's like that.
Magnificent crystals

of ice spider
across the creaking panes.

Mark Tardi

 **Bio:** Mark Tardi grew up in Chicago a scant mile away from Midway Airport. His first book, *Euclid Shudders*, was a finalist for the 2002 National Poetry Series and published by Litmus Press. More recently, two chapbooks have been released: *Part First---Chopin's Feet (G-O-N-G)*; and an excerpt from the title sequence of his new manuscript *Airport music* (Bronze Skull).

He has worked as an editor at Dalkey Archive Press, and currently he serves on the editorial board of the literary journal *Aufgabe*.

Poetic Statement:
    See: Jennifer Moxley's preface to *Imagination Verses*.

from **Airport music**

Let x equal the amount of broken glass strewn across the sidewalk;

Let y equal the most hurried, the last

this brute contingency

that any breathing falls, imperfect
half-boarded up

There's no harm for anyone else
in your mathematics

thin negatives,
slant black

never quiet, only graspless

locked into the cut of a house

Let k equal a knot of people, expectant
sounding each other out

a drawn bath to deform water

a butcher's broom

Second letter on the same day:

Best to end these confidences. It's not that I'm superstitious, but that I'm not. Some people like to go to church, and some people like cherries. A corpse won't change any of that. The usual whisper
and splash, soup and a pair of shoes.

That streets are sewn together.

Nose bleed en route.

Tray to beam.

That steak weapons.

To your desolate without.

Private fire trucks.

It's an insurance job.

Softball without gloves.

A leg laugh.

The Calumet Record, October 1907:

12 died in the neighborhood of the blast furnace;

3 were electrocuted;

1 died in a dynamite accident;

3 fell from a high place;

4 were struck by a falling object;

4 were killed by hot metal in the Bessemer department;

3 were crushed to death;

1 was suffocated by gas;

1 was thrown from a high place by the wind;

1 was scorched to death by a hot slag;

10 were killed by railroad cars or locomotives.

Yes, ruthless
so much a square mile

pickled hands and cutworm

Yes, clean geometries
successed,

warned with corners

A stuffed
zero in an armchair

poorly equipped for the cold

Your algebra nearly fainted, salt-blue

The question of specific gravity

baths filling, flagpoles
casting shadows,

your father's negative age

five years ago

5 out of 4 people have trouble with fractions.
The entireness of simple touch. All those
lost landscapes.

Your dead body looks like rain;

Mine, rotted planks for pavement, standing
water, vinegar, another flu out of season

Don't ask how we went, by what sudden leap
or what unforeseen modulation. This zero with
so many ciphers.

It was impossible to watch:

To undress and dress again.
The chest a harpsichord.

A you, cast in lost matter

Stacked tiles,
        cuttooth

as though the ridden wore nothing

no starfoot fibula,
fenced in

no contact mines

salt ready to tear the light

                    after Celan

Erica Bernheim

Bio: Erica Bernheim was born in New Jersey in 1974 and grew up in Ohio and Italy. She has studied at Miami University of Ohio; Selwyn College, Cambridge; and the Iowa Writers' Workshop. Currently, she teaches literature and writing in Chicago and is a Ph.D. candidate at the University of Illinois at Chicago. Her poems and reviews have appeared in *Black Warrior Review, Boston Review, Bridge, the Canary, Gulf Coast, the Iowa Review,* and *Volt,* most recently, and she is the Poetry Editor of *Keep Going.*

Poetic Statement:

I began as a fiction writer. And yet for me, poetry does not involve a sense of narrative the way I felt bound to it in fiction. The promise of a narrative pushes me to write each poem. I begin with a story in my mind and the most confessional of intentions. Each time, though, something happens; I am prevented from getting to the end of my story. I have to remember why a detail mattered and how it might or might not fit into what I am writing. When I wrote fiction, my characters' speech sounded to me like robots addressing each other, and in poetry, the indirect reportage I imagine in many of my own pieces feels much more natural than anything I was able to achieve in prose. I want the rush of information, the breathlessness of the line, the speed of the narrative and how it combines images with thoughts that allow for elements that do not lend themselves easily to speeding. My earliest poems were, in my mind, tremendously influenced by Robert Creeley, the poet who has most influenced my concerns with the written word. What impressed me most from a technical point of view was the apparent naturalness of his lines and enjambments, how they combined a truncated narrative confessional with contextual shifts and ongoing repositionings of the speaker. The inadequacy of language was clear through the presence of language itself, and I saw this as a liberation from the ideas I had previously entertained about the organizational "requirements" of the poem as a public object.

63rd and Pulaski

It has been you I have wanted to look at,
proving my faithfulness to my home away
from home: the appendix: something I can
live without. I had forgotten there were stars

this bright, forgotten that blocks can be
arranged and counted, their absence a reward
for sleep, their presence a reward for seizing.
The coast is gone; the ocean comes back

to us, it mouths its phosphorescence the way
destiny licks an ankle, then moves away. In
this city, seagulls greet me in the oddest places:
a supermarket parking lot, an underpass

passing for a tunnel, next to scaly pigeons
who circle finely with no shrapnel in their legs.
The seagulls whip and strain around them
by train tracks. We fall against nothing. We turn

to stone. We smolder in sunlight. Out
of respect for the gloves, the glass stays clean.
How lucky we are that others who go don't
want to come back. At noon, the grocery store

closes its doors, the sun begins to tarnish,
nights with you are not nights at all, says
one seagull to the pigeon. No, she replies,
your head goes best in the way of leaves.

Michael Antonucci

 **Bio:** Michael Antonucci's creative and critical work has appeared in a variety of publications including *African American Review, Arkansas Review, Byline, The Courtland Review,* and *Near South.* His work with The Jimmy Wynn Ensemble, the Chicago collaborative writing experiment, is found in *Admit2* and *Exquisite Corpse.* Presently, he teaches literature and writing at Marquette University in Milwaukee, Wisconsin.

Poetic Statement:

According to the figures collected by the US Census Bureau Chicago eclipsed Philadelphia as the United States' second largest city in 1890. In the span of a decade Chicago's population nearly doubled, topping 1 million inhabitants. Chicago boosters greeted the news warmly. They pointed out that city's population in1850 was at 25,000 (24th largest in the nation, just behind Lowell, Massachusetts and just ahead of Troy, New York) and anticipated continued growth into new century, predicting great things for their city.

"Bicentennial Minutes from the Vet" is an excerpt from "The Baker Bowl," a poetic cycle tracing events in Philadelphia, from the 1840s to the summer of 1976. It explores this city's ascent to and fall from Second City status.

**Bicentennial Minutes
from the Vet**

Dawning(s)
               liberty crucible
                      crack/ed
belling(s)
   cook/ed   astroturf ring/ed
      shouting(s),
thermometer   soar
candy kitchen   heat

               (for
Founding Fathers,
     Doobie Brothers,
              all sand/men

Day/ night   thicks
      reefer
      smok/ed glasses with
Mason/ite
       (Satchmo plays "Dolly"
              on Ed Sullivan:
      Wayne Twitchell is
Dixon
 warming
      in the 'pen
    Rizzo
           beef
            spew/ed into
              The Delaware
Beware
     Ben Franklin,
     cob stocked wash rooms
     President Gerald R. Ford
         (AMBIDEXTEROUS

Chris Glomski

Bio: Chris Glomski was born in Pueblo, Colorado in 1965. He grew up in Elk Grove Village, Illinois, just northwest of Chicago, attended the University of Iowa (BA, MFA), moved to Italy for a year (teaching English), and then returned to Chicago, where he has been living since. He completed a doctorate at the University of Illinois, Chicago in 2004, where he presently teaches. *Transparencies Lifted from Noon*, a first collection of poems, was published in the fall of 2005.

Poetic Statement

My habits incline to what I think of as a kind of auto-dialogue, a soliloquy uttered mainly for the chance to eavesdrop. Aware that Language poets have given us plenty of incentive to be skeptical of the lyric (or any) mode, I see my work as committed to the lyrical in an effort to project something recognizable through the film of experiences I imagine some acquaintance with. Ideally, the process would shadow a peculiar type of sensation, what the Italians call *brivido*, and the French, *frisson*, shading it with form and substance. I always find this already present in language itself. Poems in this theater may well animate epistemology, but they are not mere vehicles for it. Almost anything they have to do with knowledge is intuitive. That's why they are difficult to talk about; why they agitate before they instruct; why their lyrical trajectories arrive at "narrative" only after a time.

What will be the story of the "Third Coast" poets, who seem so together in their isolation? Accustomed to the Chicago grid, at least we understand that, before crossing the street, it makes sense to look east/west only about half the time—assuming you know where you are.

IL LA

First the flash, then the thunder.

Lying talking in bed about the rain

"I love the rain"

"And the sun makes me happy"

And the sun is hiding in the rain

"As you are hiding in your eyes"   *Why do you say that?*

Details, an uncle who called his wife "Raine"

What we're willing to say:

"Can we talk about something else now?"

Because it goes like   going back a little at a time

a day, a year, a day   to be free of it   it goes

like

First the flash, then the thunder

"Look closely at my language," Francesca Vigna said,

59

"il vetro, the masculine *glass,* goes inside *la finestra,* the feminine
window,":

                                dark-eyed, southern
                                Francesca Vigna

in inglese:
Frances Vine

Sitting staring through a window,
hours into rain that was
repeating

                "while raining, it rains."

                                Water

drips

in one of the apartments, a motor rasps
and recedes.
It is dusk all day in via della Faggiola, 12.
As in the old film effect, the one in which the clock
hands swim round and round the dial through a cross-eyed lens,
this day winds by each window of the house. First
the street at noon, men pulling their huge straw
brooms like oars, packs of schoolchildren, day-glo
knapsacks bobbing behind them as they maneuver toward

the Leaning Tower.
Enter the washed light of my room, the ivy breathes
on the walls outside. Then the street again at mid-afternoon,
deserted, an occasional voice, a footfall, wind.
When the real hour of dusk has finally swung round,
between two of the bars on my window a strand
of cobweb vibrates, is stretched back like a bow, then sags again;
it doesn't break. Nothing has changed: nothing
has stopped changing.

On the Lungarno, her fuck-all stride, tossing all that hair,
        *ciao*ing a stranger, Francesca, her vine.

when they turn

I know there must be some truth there,

                    for so many to see something *in me*

                        it must be there,

it's how I know my—

"I hafta meet my pusher in the piazza dei miracoli."

Through a window:
Blue Line train, morning, January, Monday

Chicago
Ci cago

through

                            headlights rushing from
an overpass and dopplering by the guard-rails

Chain-link rust

                            & faces
                            on the platform
                            full of winter

                            "Addison will be next"

Tires flinging up ice

                            bulbs in sequence
                            across a marquee

1 (800) COLLISION

                            What was

through the little window
I have to you, the glass?

A CLEAR DAY IS HERE

the you the

Water tank sky
Starling struck

SIDNEY SHELDON: NOTHING LASTS FOREVER

The life paint of your face's grip on you,
the paint of the life of a face---

                              almost illegible, only

First a flash

in a supermarket, a winter sun through storefront
lays glow on
a mesh of oranges being scanned, oranges held in a woman's hands
& how

dizzy with   *What you*

dragged   a little, back, like through a window,

Until   again

June, morning, the day's hot forecast
trudging through screens into bedroom

to be

beaten into breezes by ceiling fan into whose
whirling blades my thoughts on green bed sheets tumbled:

dumb joy of an oldies station straining under your unconscious
sing-along,

smoothing your clothes with an iron warm as the day would nearly
be

the room is you
smoothing your shirt
and you and the song

rolling green within the walls

                              & outside the supermarket

carrying the oranges
tires flinging up ice

everyone is alone
in their car
on the heart

                         of thunder

a flash becomes

When in the morning sun-up strikes a kitchen,

haloes whole the window above sink, bringing out the full

yellow brilliance in a bottle of dish soap

whose label reports

If Dawn gets in

your eyes, rinse

with water

Vigils of the Fire

Circle burns, waiting for someone to come
Garden of tucked sleeves, spore finding his
eye; embryos tear lashes from sparks
         in a womb

                  blasphemous phosphene
                         vacancy   Think it is real

Awake something wicked, in formaldehyde—
                  vigils of the fire, totem named Shantih

orders your glass face   eroded by a mistress

who's been in the fire
and sucks red coal   the vigil is as even
                                   as fire—it is parity

Could you not stay awake one hour?

                         Skirting open-ended
florally, loathe to whitewash being
as plucked inward there came challenges to flowers
  Something reeling carried itself to couch,
         shrank before new views, then couldn't
         get up

unless down shook trees' to new shushing
for what something might be about

as sudden a vigil by style as danger involved to alter

the red sentence burning is certainly about, its phrase
a fire pushing into the gym, a balance that takes in
a whole world until scale is a vigil by
        fire inside you

It Wants to Go to Bed with Us

A laundromat. That suited, halted man, halted
but smiling----   who eased into, then
backed off, street. His hat. Zoom. Hangers.

This must be the beginning of the great disappointments,
perspiring and dolorous, mean
as meaningless twilight. Who basks

between our ears? Meaning you.
Dying, eh? (In the end there is, um, the end.) Cinders
in the eye, piecemeal, it was. Are you relaxed?

Hair tosses. We are mostly leaving,
slantways, doorways, going like evening into a lake.
Sounding the blood into night.

Kept stopping for a while, like if I'd forgotten, but that

shirt's done. It's done, and I won't take it with me.

Garin Cycholl

Bio: Garin Cycholl is author of *Blue Mound to 161* (Pavement Saw Press) and *Nightbirds* (Moria Books). He teaches writing and literature at the University of Illinois at Chicago.

Poetic Statement

The poems here engage photographs done by Aaron Siskind in the mid-20th century. Photography generally engages me as a poet, because like the poem, the photograph marks a point of slippage between public and private space. The public spaces here are cityscapes: a truck parked under a Chicago overhead ("Chicago 53") and a pier diver moving through the air ("Levitations"). Of course, within the photographer's eye, these are also private spaces, again made public in the instant of captured light. Similarly, the poem marks a moment of transition between spaces, the serious play of the public dimensions of geography and city with the poem's field of memory and imagination.

In his essay, "The Drama of Objects," Siskind evidenced "the desire to see the world clean and fresh and alive, as primitive things are clean and fresh and alive." In the photographs poemed above, the truck is parked not only under a city overhead, but also on prairie along an expressway that cuts the city into distinct spaces, north/south, black/white. The pier diver begins not only a descent towards water, but also turns in a plunge into the "pleasures and terrors" of Cold War America. As such, the poem in general is able to reconnect public and private spaces. In a moment where most public language seems bent on severing memory from history and life from land, the poem is the fertile space in which the tissues of memory and history are reunited.

Chicago 53

after Aaron Siskind

the mind into torn paper;
the sound stranded there—
take your guitar to the West
Side, tune it under the neon
canopy   the wires
stretched tight where the
first shots were fired

                    "there
is only the drama of objects
and you, watching"

2

        (how the frame fits

ex: the 1919 World Series as con-
fidence game   but any more so than
brick & glass, Ceres herself?

Shoeless Joe and Happy
Felsch were sportively dressed
in gray silk shirts, white duck
trousers and white shoes   they
came down the steps slowly,
their faces masked by impassivity

the texture of memory is never
brick or paint, light cracked and
prairied

                the rock's skin,
the knothole resisting black
paint—throw a light at it and it

69

burns   CARTAGE below
Chryslers moving west

          "not some whitebread cartel"

3

unconscious for days, the city

          (or better, hand tracings

you begin to think of it as
"America"   *primitive things,*
clean fresh & alive—the dancers are
gone, handbooked into concrete
and rust, jazz peeled from the
façade

               all that happens
here happens in secret—the
dedication of this concrete this
tree, it grows at night—this country
exists in oblivion—the paint blown
or clawed, the third baseman awaiting
the throw   in the ground, we
ate light

                    memory gone
into the "paper of tomorrow"

          (light into motion

Jesus turns on the radio; he likes
AM, the big sound of wax
          "history
is the swamp of many foundations"

4

or the city as a series of collapsing
right angles, blacked and whited
against sky   resisting blue
or "Red Door, Green Building" in-
viting shadow—*we track our own
desire*—oblivion is not some drama

if you believe the brick is corrupted,
what about the glass?   "representation
of a deep need for order" a line drawn
in green water   Fred Hampton and
Mark Clark moving through the West
Side

              *eventually the story
will become glorified and the facts
more harmoniously fitted together—*

5

"when the surrealists discovered
this country, they pushed the rail-
roads west of the Mississippi"

another piece of the puzzle   he
hands you the phonebook, a paper
stele along the road   the Dan Ryan
is concrete, cut into the ground

                              (it
grows secretly at night, light flashed
as language—what's left of the city,
"the x of it"

Levitations

after Aaron Siskind

to read these put your
head in a tuck—your
shoulders in a box
the masks tangible
as air muscles plied
into frame then
grayed *the*

       sky gives way
staring into your own
shoulder (not as solid as
it seemed
       tell your knees
you love the sky   the
sadness realizing Hi is
dead   the letters have
stopped coming but you
now a story of falling
bodies splashing into
the air below your hip
gives way to it
explodes
       and

what's on the water?
paper greased and alumi-
nummed down and
greened your fingers
splitting it—a hands
down myth here
counting ribs
through

surface

flying

into a silvered
gelatin skin your
consciousness is a
helicopter whirl
thrown against
a brickpile

you rise to
the applause of
towheaded kids on
the pier and tell
yourself *that's*
America

Luis Urrea

Bio: Luis Alberto Urrea is the token Mexican of Naperville, Illinois. "The Signal-to-Noise Ratio" comes from a new book of poems, *Songs of the Sacrificial Class*. He is the author of *The Devil's Highway* and *The Hummingbird's Daughter*. He teaches at University of Illinois Chicago.

Poetic Statement

In the darkest moments of my life—both as a person and as a writer—I was in Tucson, Arizona. No career, no relationships, no money, no food. All the things I knew and trusted lost to me—even the woman I thought I would marry. I was in alien territory, researching *The Hummingbird's Daughter*. I was reading a lot of haiku. Probably, my mind could only absorb 17 syllables in its torments. But there was a deep comfort in the poems, especially the poems of Issa. Issa suffered a lot of terrible things, but his work exploded with joy. And Issa had a simple rule: Trust. I did not know what to trust, so I chose to trust Issa! And, later, when I found myself in Chicago, I believed I had made a bad mistake. I couldn't find any magic or Grace here. Where were the saguaros? Where were the Yaqui medicine women? But ol' Issa was here, too. And Chicago started to reveal its own poetry to me. It wasn't Carl Sandburg's poetry, either. No, we're funkier than that now. We're alive with scary clouds rolled in from Iowa and far South Dakota. We're haunted by late night strangers—foxes sneak in from the suburbs. I have a wild turkey that came from somewhere and lives in my back yard. I saw a tumbleweed rolling down Ogden. Chicago had all these mysteries that Issa would have laughed at and praised. And, in trust, I decided to praise them, too.

The Signal-to-Noise Ratio: Chicago Haiku

Jackson & Harlem

I will fuck you up.
Come back here motherfucker.
You 'bout to get served.

#

Ogden & Western

Oil change and filter—
$39 Special!
Coffee and donuts.

#

Sun-Times

Killed wife, girl, in-laws—
Several hard hammer blows—
Insulted manhood.

#

WLS

I'm the decider.
Conservative Compassion.
I'm the uniter.

#

Grant Park

Pigeon on the ice

Picking at yellow vomit
Of homeless soldier.

#

South Loop

Do I transfer here
To catch the Orange Line?
I'll get fired for sure.

#

Austin & Roosevelt

Paletas frescas!
Tacos, tortas, menudo!
Go back home, beaner!

#

Biograph

Lady in Red's ghost
Can't escape alley's mouth:
Johnny Dillinger.

#

South Racine

Why you stone trippin'
Babygirl I aint pimpin'—
Got your back for reals.

#

Airport

Security check:
Remove your shoes and jackets.
Welcome to O'Hare.

#

Millennium Park

Do you know Jesus?
If you were to die tonight
Would you go to Heaven?
#

Proviso East High School

Hallways full of ghosts
From Chicago to Detroit—
No Child Left Behind.

Kristy Odelius

Bio: Kristy Odelius is a poet and Assistant Professor of English at North Park University (Chicago, IL) where she teaches poetry and 19th century British literature. She is a co-founder of *Near South*, a Chicago-based journal of innovative writing. Her poems, essays and reviews have appeared or are forthcoming in *Notre Dame Review, Chicago Review, Combo, Versal, ACM, Pavement Saw, La Petite Zine, Diagram,* and others.

Poetic Statement:

In short, I'm with Stevens, whose work suggests that lyric poets are "thinkers without final thoughts." Like it or not-of course I like it-I find myself firmly situated in that lyric tradition. I often return to the rhetorical punch of Sappho, the metaphysically "wicked" Dickinson, and the lofting locations of Guest to induce bouts of pleasurable thinking. Many of my poems (via a variety of she-speakers) address the intellectual, domestic, and perception-based experiences of women. The splendor of poetics is best turned on the poems of others; ultimately our poems-not our professed poetics-reveal the Things We Can't Resist.

The Virgins of Chicago

work nights at "Federal Screw
Products." They like welding,
sweating and wearing
gray aprons.

"I can't feel anything,"
I sigh as the elevator rises.
The meta-galaxy slips
like a ring on my finger,
a parenthesis squeezing the night
in towards morning.

They rest in the caliper,
thinking about tree
trunks, project their
cool measure, summon
the helicopter.

The sky pales, a weird ochre.
All yellow, I'm flying an octave
below the shareholders. It's
always the same. I remember
their names. I can't see their faces,
I can't read their folders.

Cardio/sky

And when the reds arrive moving as if toward a name
Or a distant cabana, zero in on a shelter
As a generation glides with ignorance and grace

Cloud-crack around twist to a peak
                              lie in the sand alone

Blood vessels stretched to shade
Tuning what the sky slips on over itself
A cask spilled out, colorific-in-time

There's no consummation

Waves slap shore wet and wet and wet
There's no consumption, only being
consumed, an imbroglio imbued with reds

We stroke without contact our delicate imbalance
Panama Red, red letter, red meat or stumble upon

Redivivus
Redivivus come back
Come back to life

Thoughts of Falling, Pollen, Pare
after Sappho

When champion-bred
leaves lie splayed
like minimum wage
sin, when sleep,
a raincoat czar,
spreads its liquid
hands thin, I'll say
      not on: *your life, your daddy's knee, a new knife blade.*

Try, swim the brackish margin
between holy and hole, the ocean's
backstitched locomotion loosely
recites "no, there's no such
night in prosaic blood" nodding
its great nose toward the
mollusky dance-floor.

When honey leaks from
eyes bent to breezes
eyes like peach pits
fragrant and useless,

the czar disappears into
the rain's rumpled plumage
my heart's gong-bruised knees
buckling through branches.

It's bee-spit
that blows me
      I admit
and you
away.

Simone Muench

 **Bio:** Simone Muench grew up in
Louisiana and Arkansas before
moving to Colorado to receive her BA
and MA from the University of
Colorado. Her first book *The Air Lost
in Breathing* won the Marianne Moore
Prize for Poetry (Helicon Nine, 2000).
Her second *Lampblack & Ash* received
the Kathryn A. Morton Prize for Poetry (Sarabande Books, 2005),
and was one of the editor's selections in the *New York Times* Book
Review. She has poems appearing in *Iowa Review, Poetry, American
Poet, Caffeine Destiny, Dusie,* and others. She received her Ph.D.
from the University of Illinois at Chicago, and is an assistant
professor and director of the Writing Program at Lewis University.
Currently, she serves on the advisory board for Switchback Books,
is a contributing editor to *Sharkforum.org* where she presents a
"poem of the week" series, and is an avid horror film fan.

Poetic Statement:

> Only one thing remained reachable, close and secure amid
> all losses: language.—Celan

Writing that guides me often navigates the intangible space
when self becomes other; when identity becomes identities; when
landscape and self are interpenetrated; when one is suspended in
the cross-gaps of history and memory, dreaming and waking,
elucidation and mystification. I gravitate toward crepuscular
dreamscapes where metamorphoses, the marvelous and the bizarre
occur. I'm under the spell of horror films and Surrealism. I think of
them as related in their refusal to engage in binary thinking, laying
claim instead to ambivalence and ambiguity, to the eros that rises
out of and above erosion, and to Todorov's "the fantastic"—the
threshold between the explainable and the inexplicable.

I tend to think of poems as collaborative acts, as calls-and-
responses, as dedicatory. I like the acts of accretion a poem
partakes in, its palimpsestic nature. I don't subscribe to "anxiety of

influence," I am illumined by influence: the South's flora/fauna, musicians Howe Gelb and Tim Rutili, metaphor's associative logic, film noir, the erotica of pre-code Hollywood, *Meshes of the Afternoon*, dead girls, Cortazar, Carter, Stevens, Neruda, and Desnos. As well as female surrealists, like Joyce Mansour and Leonora Carrington, and their commitment toward transfiguring "woman" as object into agent, recuperating her from the era's slotbox of cypher. In terms of poetic creation, it comes down to Atwood's adage that "a word after a word after a word is power." As far as the reception part, Frank O'Hara has the final say: "if they don't need poetry bully for them."

Viewing Rain from a Hospital Bed

after Levertov

Something sidles
up to me in the dark, I

taste it; this disease
I can't speak.

I listen to rain, tangled
branches, scar on my chest.

It shoots. You
lick it.

How is it? Don't go
where you don't belong.

It's how you hear it—
scar, emblem of chance,

unnamable odor
pearling out of it

and over you,
stifling you in bed.

But what if
like an axolotl, its

quickness I visit,
and slip coiling into light?

Not scar, not
that voice

of ache and tomorrow; or bone
crack for having moved too fast.

What if held beneath sea
it turned a beautiful

blue, an impenetrable
blue? Could all that liquid

be the source of fall?
Here beneath flesh: is an I

with diamond bones, some
split in rot, others

rain sparks, sage
blooming additions. Here it ends—

could I erase
in lampblack rain,

the moon flickering?

By Your Mouth

At night I sleep with the saddest men

but today I ache, moths and blood
decorating my bed, a conjuring

trick I shrink
my spine into. My wrists

raw wool and black
as malpractice from your bite.

Today, not even a meteor swarm
can alarm me.

My hands bare the bad lands,
molded riot of Texas

purple spike. Debut of the mad
muse—how like spies it is disguised.

Outdoors, the wars roar on and
the dead are gathered

like promissory notes and buried
in their grandmothers' mink coats.

◊

You salute with a broken tooth, words
tapering off, vapor lifting out your eyes,
no longer knowing the difference between
photographs and mirrors. Shadows border
lips, the severe sheerness of your existence.
Call in the maintenance staff for your removal.
You're a groove in my lineage, a greasy spoon
where I consumed eggs overeasy. The sun's
just a rerun. I'd come to your funeral

if I were in a better mood, but my head jerks
with a thousand whipsnakes. When you died,
I swooned like a flamenco dancer on Acapulco
gold while honey guides and vinegar flies gathered
near your stain, small as bird shadow, on the snow.

◊

Days when I gaze into your glass
eye, archeological remains

of your tortured back, mustangs
gather at your open mouth.

You conspire against my pleasure,
your sadness is ferocious, taller

than Kilimanjaro. You live in my ribs,
a ruby boutonnière; you are plum

and pendulum; a car salesman in white
tie and tails. You're bizarre as innards,

buzzards as you stumble dream
to dream you reside in margins,

in the blurry vision of virgins;
in my eyes, you are aniline dye,

the deep south of your contagious mouth.

One Swallow Doesn't Make a Summer

1.   A poem is
cuttlebone. Sugarcube.
It's a fiction. A glass of milk.

Baudelaire's concubine. An eager
sugar. A lunar reader.
A diary tax. Conflation of cupboard
and springboard. Conquistador and concerto.
A way of happening, a mouth. A landscape
drowsy, full of contradictions and peach trees.
A song, an urn, the ashcan
of imagine. Glass spittoon, a broken
arm. The elegance of the letter *f*.
Green noise of teeth, their
clackclack at night when the maids
are sleeping.

2.   Poem marry me.
My absinthe bride-to-be
bury me in a barn with hair
husks, pollen dust.
Your eyes chasuble blue.
Sugar beet stench around your neck.
Widow cluster. Working
on the curtains, the wedding-ring quilts.
You quit us. And I was glad.
With your sad magnetic face around your aging lace.

3.   Poetry's two-
lipped, sloe-black
and cobalt. Spasmodic.
Her bakelite bracelets
jangling. *Random patterning*
within a simple phenomenal system.
Sipping slivovitz on the terrace, she was
seized with *mal de mer* though she wasn't at sea.

4.   Shush.
The windows are waking us
from revisionist dreams. Maize light
raising us from deep sea sleep.
Your words are seaspray,
agave. You are wafer weight

in my lightning mouth. I burn you
to strawberry. Leaf-lake. Glass bird
don't break.

Lea Graham

Bio: Lea Graham was born in Memphis, Tennessee and grew up in Northwest Arkansas. She has lived in Missouri, New Jersey, Chicago, the Dominican Republic and Costa Rica. She is currently Writer in Residence at Clark University in Worcester, Massachusetts where she teaches Creative Writing-Poetry, Literature and Travel Writing.

Her chapbook, *Calendar Girls*, was published by above/ground Press in March 2006. Her poetry and translations have been published in journals such as *Notre Dame Review*, *The Worcester Review*, *Mudlark*, *Moria*, and *Shadow Train*. She serves as an associate editor of the Chicago journal, *Near South*.

Poetic Statement:

I am interested in a poetry that is able, as Louise Glück wrote, "to harness the power of the unfinished." Poems that use the space around them, silence, ellipses and fragments have an enormous attraction for me. The suggestion of what might happen or what might have happened is more interesting to me than what did. Like briefly catching bars of an old song as you pass a doorway, what is evoked by the partial is charged with possibility and mystery. I think about this when writing my own poems even as I deal in the "stuff" that makes up place and the richness of geographies.

Crush # 77

Hand's gesture

patterns   eyes' catch:
          the Apollo   between

ring finger   and heart line

turns
      palm's lovely

heft at neck,   Sparks

axon,   signals:

Let's go   drive 'til   morning comes...

Nones/January

I tell him "wine has no rudder" & so
we drink vodka tonics, watch the motions

of a bay: *See how the current now moves
out,* a sweet broom of moustache into

a collar. My face buried just above
the occipital bone, breathing earth &

summer hay, a small nest & respite
from cold in the 18th hour. We fidget

in rough sheets, a dry heat. I tell him stories
of sex with other men to stop from—   O

90

double-bearded Janus, the way winter
lies around us

The Rushing

Forsythia at roadside
arcing up,

a reach for
what? Passing on foot or in

reluscent car— past already—
so brilliant

a wanting
and yet. Yearning already

for the next before bloom: Love,
perhaps, or

not love— but
its desire, things as Michael

might say, *Turning…on and off
and on* stems'

phloem, lenticels, xylem,
this old wood

flowering

Ed Roberson

Bio: Ed Roberson grew up in Pittsburgh, Pennsylvania. He did undergraduate research in Limnology, with expeditions to Alaska, the Aleutians, and Bermuda. He also worked as a diver training porpoises in the *Pittsburgh Aquazoo* public aquarium, at an advertising graphics agency, and in steel mills. He has climbed mountains in the Peruvian and Ecuadorian Andes and explored the upper Amazon jungle. He also motorcycled across the USA, and traveled in Mexico, the Caribbean, and Nigeria.

Roberson has published seven books of poetry, one of which was a winner of the Iowa Poetry Prize, and another in the National Poetry Series Competition. *Atmosphere Conditions* (2000) was nominated by the Academy of American Poets for the Lenore Marshall Award. He also received the Lila Wallace Reader's Digest Writer's Award and his work has appeared in the *Pushcart Prize* and *Best American Poetry.* He has taught poetry at the University of Pittsburgh, Rutgers College, Rutgers University, and the Dodge Foundation Poetry Festival. Recently retired from Rutgers, Roberson has just completed an appointment as Visiting Artist at Columbia College Chicago and is an adjunct at Northwestern University.

Poetic Statement:

At the moment, it feels as though I'm being re-introduced to poetry. Or this may be a version of the feeling that each new poem is a new definition of poetry, a new statement of poetics. Either way, the moment of writing – and also of reading a good poem – is one in which I regain balance.

Sight Read of a Couple of Stars

A couple of stars late
            arriving into place,
    but these are the morning's
            traffic helicopters hanging;

the stage lights lit along
            the bottom of the curtain,
    the reddening
            Lake Michigan horizon.

The lake's line, which the downbeat
            for the day makes its baton
    strike up the water to the sky
            on, opens

the world suite we play in on
            time, or our   missed cue,   wherever
    we come in, our
            origin we don't understand making

as to achieve creation on
            arrival, to hit it
    where we hit it right
            on time: the song on

point
            by point, note by note
    the improvisation;
            a score star by star –

the lights on the cars
            down Lake Shore Drive
    – of the galaxial journey.

(*from* City Eclogue)

When the Morning Come

This high up always felt like suicide
I felt it in my balls when I looked down
face against the window   a reflex action
of muscle to a sense of danger

It abruptly withdraws the testicles
to safety   It hurts   a cramp in the groin
never quite distinguishing between the nature
of survival and a yearning for it over with ...

never quite sorted out ...
I had that problem, so I ...
But here they are   *come together as one*
(a line from the hymn "*'Bye And 'Bye*") and not a choice

anymore of jumping   or adjusting to the fire
when the morning come.

Well,   bye 'n bye   when the morning come
All the saints   well   get together as one
We will tell the story   how it all begun
We will understand it better bye 'n bye

Not Brought Up

Just as a matter of scope it felt
    like that
    was the numbers of people
we wanted justice
    brought down upon –
    that many gone along
keeping silent kept in office for –
    Just the sweep of the complicit terror
    against us –

The lynchings each   of the thousands of
    times it happened
    the whole white town
come down
    to a smoky picnic –   each black
    blackened by the family there is in soot
must have felt that
    magnitude against them   stacked
    high   come down out of the hills

must have felt that
    register   force   the running
    or the blank walk   away
up Broadway or Greenwich
    coated in the white   no longer
    simple ash   ghosts   like a range of that
not brought up

Arielle Greenberg

Bio: Arielle Greenberg is the author of *My Kafka Century* (Action Books, 2005) and *Given* (Verse, 2002) and the chapbook *Farther Down: Songs from the Allergy Trials* (New Michigan, 2003). Her poems have been included the 2004 and 2005 editions of *Best American Poetry* and a number of other anthologies, including *Legitimate Dangers* (Sarabande, 2006). She is the poetry editor for the journal *Black Clock* and a founder and co-editor of the journal *Court Green*. She is an Assistant Professor in the poetry program at Columbia College Chicago and lives in Evanston, IL with her family.

Poetic Statement:

In my first book, I was seeking to allow myself permission to be playful, messy, funny—to risk failure, as a true experiment should. My second book was an attempt to address issues I felt I'd been avoiding and needed to face—issues of selfhood, of anger, of cultural and historical legacy—without making poems that were didactic, overtly representational, or humorless.

After the birth of my daughter, my poems became more direct and urgent, I think: I had less time and energy for games in my work than I once did. Now this, too, is slowly starting to change. My poetic project is the project of the life I'm living, which is to say I have little control over where it might need to go next.

Hotel

We know. The rooms seem empty.
Our names are in the most lost registers.
We were given a system to cut the life from our mouth.
Or no system. Either way a scream.

All the sheets here are white,
with behind-the-black faces.
You can do a thing with a faucet,
a concussion. This nation knows to bruise.

Death is a very close door in the hall—
see how our foot slips in?
(The sweet taste of shit.)
See how everything, history, is a chute?
See how our tongue, this close door,
is also that black, that sweet?

Fuck us in springtime.
Let the air roll over the mass grave like petals.
It also smells sweet. It is our hair.
It is chalk, bags of rice, nails.

There is a star here called America.
We follow her everywhere.
She is a ball of gas,
a fired-off round, a stove, a blackout.
She keeps us in her kitchen.

We could be anyone.
Under the bed, we are anyone.
Any genocide we've mentioned.

The Missing, The Maybe

I.   When they took from me the rotten tooth
I asked them to take, I asked
it back, so I could palm and size the hole,
see the dead grey place on the slick bone.
So I could keep whole, keep all I own.

Made from a promise of sand,
of stars, I wash away with just wind.
These bones my sail-bones.
These teeth my anchors.

II.   This is the central text:
middle of the book with its white silk thread
cut through like a tooth,
middle of the page, flocked with red comment.
These words have been here before.
History is a spell spelled with dust.

III.   Black witch, white witch.

Do not let anyone steal away with your hair.
Anything from your body can be used to make you weak.

Do not ink the skin that belongs to God, borrower.
It must return as it came, like clean sheets.

Perfume the house with sage, the oven
with salt. Burn your leavened germs to dust.

IV.   Yes, another book about genocide
and my body. And the third element
I cannot recall: tell me again, was it wind?

V.   To make art, I sleep with the face
of another white woman on my face.
To trick the spirits. To redden
their eyes. To keep
my child (I do not have) alive in its rocking bed
I sleep in this glass box like the woman
with the poison apple, waiting without breath. Someone
may make an image of it, but the soul will fly up.
I will curl into my white mask,
an angel in the death-house.

VI.   What of the salted ovens?

VII.   I am meat

(blood, rib lifted from man and sand).
I remember this by keeping an animal at the foot of my bed
like an amulet. We are neither
of us fit for burning. None.

VIII.   Here is the thing about teeth:
they last a long enamel.

Sixty years is a mere mother, nothing.

Germany is a very pretty continent
I will never see, a grey place in the back of my mouth.

Poland, Austria.
I am halfway to sixty, halfway to an attic.

IX.   Before the woman with the poison apple,
there was a shrieker made from no rib.
God took her back by the hair.

White ghost, red ghost.

They took her bone white child.
Left her with a gaping mouth.

X.   Now they have excised the smallest bones
from my feet and I did not remember
to ask them back so I could keep them. Unwhole,
I can be screwed to a post,
possessed, known by my breath to be this yellow star girl.

I keep an animal with me like an Eden,
for protection. From God. From history. From the spells.
Me and her, we speak with the same black tongue.

Robyn Schiff

Bio: Originally from New Jersey, Robyn Schiff holds an MFA from the Iowa Writers' Workshop and an MA in medieval studies from the University of Bristol, in England. She has taught at the University of Oregon and Northwestern University, and lives in Andersonville, Chicago with her husband, the poet Nick Twemlow. Schiff is editor-at-large for the journal *The Canary*, and her first book, *Worth*, was published in 2002 by University of Iowa Press, Kuhl House Poets. Her second book, *51*, is forthcoming from the same press in 2008.

Poetics Statement:
"Colt Rapid Fire Revolver" was written during the last few weeks before we became engaged in the war, and was the first poem I wrote for my new manuscript, a collection of poems that in part regards objects that were on display at The Great Exhibition of 1851 in England. The poems in this manuscript are political and personal, and concern themselves with how the objects we create incriminate us in ineffable acts of betrayal. This is a collection of corporate histories, indictments, fantasias, and apologies, and I'm interested in how the formal unit of the sentence can organize and disorganize its content as it violently weaves through the arbitrary stanzaic arrangements of the poems.

Colt Rapid Fire Revolver

The wedding cake of Elizabeth Hart (Colt since
noon) was trimmed with sugar pistols
with revolving sweet-tooth chambers with gears
that rotate one position over like a
dancer down a dance line
prompted by an aisle that parts in music
to switch partners while a

fly drawn to the sugar places a stringy foot
on the trigger. Dysentery.
There must be a gallery with bull's-eyes
blown through sugar faces spun on the same scale
and a wife at a sewing
bee bridging a scarf like a ray of house-
fly regurgitation

between her sticky knitting needles who admits
that when her husband said he'd be
at the gallery she assumed he meant
to see pictures she was too innocent to
see. She imagined him hat
in hand leaning toward a battle scene and
deep in the grainy wound

in the painting's newly dead, indeed a bullet
too deep to see gleams beyond the
vanishing point in both his vision as
he aims and fires in target practice and hers
as she conjures past a line
she would never cross on foot following
the caravan of her

thinking in tedious steps over internal
prairie until it overcomes
the body of her youngest catching
a fly off an ox's tail while the
oxen are moving and yet

onward the party continues until
the provisions of her

fantasy wear thin. Though this is manifest in
sugar, it still disturbs me when
the Donner Party built to scale with the
Patented Colt Revolvers trimming this cake
melt their weakest into a
desperate sap. Though the world's first sugar
bowl was passed from guest to

guest to show the wealth of Elizabeth's court when
an ounce of sugar traded for
a calf, it's worth more than that. You demur
to mourn lives lost in the frontier raised in scale
and substance to people the
West the Patented Colt Revolvers that
trim a cake were cast to

defend, but I say the bull's-eyes marksmen see mapped
upon the apples poised on the
heads of all things are cut on a lathe whose
smallest revolution of thought is in sync
with that which shapes the metal
of the revolving chamber whose circular
machinations synchronize

with the rings a fly circling the bullet wound
makes in air. Focus my gaze; I
see like a fly whose vision is more like
several interlocking rings left by a tea-
cup on a book but the cake
was six feet high and how could I resist
pistols winding tier up-

on tier up the icing reverberating in
decoration the prudence of
a revolvers' placement in the holsters
of a row of guards under whose raised arms that

beam a private arbor the
bride and bridegroom enter their union. Re-
petition of pistols

map a rebus of progress marching since the first
firearms to devise a weapon
that can repeat fire without reloading.
Behold the rapid fire pistol inspired
by Colt's meditations on
the wheel of the ship steering him toward
India spinning and

locking in position like the machinations
of fortune pacing through the in-
finite face of its clock in such baby
steps that I shall reign I reign I reigned adjust
the powers of judgement en-
trusted to calibrate them. Leaning in
to see the gears, like the

wick of one candle used to light the next all along
a dark corridor, leaning in
and replicating, is not unlike the vision
the sugar wife had of her sugar husband
leaning in to see the detail
of a battle painting,
and stirred by the fire there,
enlisting.

Nick Twemlow

Bio: Originally from Topeka, Kansas, Nick Twemlow holds an MFA from the Iowa Writers' Workshop, and an MA from New Zealand's International Institute of Modern Letters, where he was a Fulbright Fellow. He serves as co-editor of *The Canary*, and his poems have been published in *A Public Space, Boston Review, Denver Quarterly, Fence, Volt,* and elsewhere. He directed a short film that played in several film festivals, including the Tribeca Film Festival. He is at work on a manuscript of poems called "Damage Manual" and a screenplay for a martial arts film entitled "Tapped Out." He lives in Andersonville, Chicago with his wife, the poet Robyn Schiff.

Poetics Statement:
I'm interested in the play between intense psychological states and flat affect. I'm curious about the mind at work—by which I mean two things: how does the mind move from A to B in a violent world, but moreover, how do we respond to endless hours of workaday boredom. The literal and symbolic water coolers and cubicle walls lit by fluorescent track lighting and filled with employee banter typify the modern asylum of a downtown office with lake views. I'm also fascinated by our intense surveillance of each other and how well prepared we are to be surveilled. Thus the form of the cubicle, its derangement, the intersection of words like 'spider' and 'hole,' the contemplation of such things while sitting in a faux Herman Miller Aeron chair, surfing, checking various inboxes, watching pixilated cell footage of a dictator being hanged, mash-ups of a Canadian teen wielding a light saber, home video of a child's face engulfed in the back blow of birthday cake candles gone screwy.

Foreign Affairs

Spear hand to the sternum. Cross shuto
to the ribs. You want to locate
the precise moment when a reverse punch
to the face might enfeeble
an army of shit-serious anarchists
hell-bent on keeping the withering sanctions
intact. Back knuckle to the groin'll
show 'em. Ridge hand to the temple.
A necklace of ears & a hammer fist
god damn square on the bridge of the nose.
Solder x/y to otherwise sexless
killing machines. Double fist to the
ribs & groin. Repeat these secret strikes
like you've got privilege
coursing through your veins. Back
knuckle to the face. Bend & flex
the arm with all the grace you place
the dessert fork above the dinner plate.
Double shuto to the neck and ribs.
Ridge hand to the groin. Six-year-old
kid smiles senile when uppercut
to the jaw blows his fecal
little village to pieces. He's got
the shakes & being taught spear hand
to the bladder he understands how a flower
morphs into a daisy cutter & how
thin the line between. Straight up shuto to the face.
It's basics. Like diplomacy. Like a palm heel
to the heart. Buckle up little shell shocked
son of some gladly erased.

A Land Without Flowers of Near Distances

Lead me to the spiderhole
Let me love the wonderful
News of spiderholes
Discovered in parts heretofore
Parts unknown the ones that groan
Spiderhole of my dream
Nightmare reduction
I like your pincers
Spiderhole and a mule the promise
I take to mean I'm free
I love how it's prepared medium rare
Consider shadow
Of spiderhole your own
Very I'm very concerned about the war
I own too many spiderholes not to be
I bought spiderholes when nobody else would
Touch them
Dank lack of love
Dank hole in head
Sting owns spiderholes in Spain
When I treble high
Some sick I gather
To make better friends
Cold in spiderhole
Money enough to think freedom's within reach

Tony Trigilio

Bio: Born in Erie, Pennsylvania, to an immigrant family who worked in factory, mining, and farming communities, Tony Trigilio has lived most of his life in Chicago and Boston. Trigilio earned a Ph.D. in English and Poetics from Northeastern University, Boston, in 1997, and moved to Chicago in 1998. Since 1999, he has taught in the English Department at Columbia College Chicago, where he serves as Director of Creative Writing—Poetry.

Trigilio is the author of a collection of poems, *The Lama's English Lessons* (Three Candles Press, 2006). His poems have been published in many journals, and in recent anthologies such as *Digerati: 20 Contemporary Poets in the Virtual World* (Three Candles, 2006) and *America Zen* (Bottom Dog Press, 2004). He co-edits (with Arielle Greenberg and David Trinidad) the poetry journal *Court Green,* published in association with Columbia College Chicago. Trigilio also is the author of two books of criticism: a study of Allen Ginsberg's Buddhist poetry, *Allen Ginsberg's Buddhist Poetics* (Southern Illinois University Press, forthcoming 2007), and an exploration of poetry and prophecy, *"Strange Prophecies Anew": Rereading Apocalypse in Blake, H.D., and Ginsberg.* He is one of the founding members of The Beat Studies Association, and serves on its board.

Poetic Statement:
Poetry forces me to pay attention – probably more than any other art form does, though music comes very close. It forces me to be patient, to slow down my intellectual and emotional attention spans and really listen to the languages around me. I write from anxiety, too, a fear that some part of the world might go unrepresented unless it's shaped into language. I grew up in a household and extended family where a couple different languages were spoken, English and Italian, so I was fortunate to be exposed at an early age to all the ways language can fail to convey anything. My mother suffered from terrible hearing loss, and we took it for

granted in our family that language flops as often as it succeeds. We talked all the time anyway. The colloquial oral histories my family told over dinner and at reunions had a great effect on me – especially when I couldn't make "sense" from stories of how they navigated this strange new country and how their other-ness unsettled them. When I was in junior high, a friend and I created our own phonetic alphabet because we were frustrated by the difference between the spoken and written word. I still compose first drafts of poems in this alphabet, a great way to hear the words as early as possible in the drafting. So when I really started to study language, as both a poet and scholar, it wasn't so esoteric to think of words as trustworthy and fickle at the same time. It was actually quite personal.

I'm attracted equally to narrative and procedural forms. We don't always admit this, but good narrative is full of associational logic and the multiple voices of collage – and it inspires trust in the representational at the same time it reminds us that representations are fictions. My background in music, especially avant-garde forms, exerts a huge influence on my experiments with language and form in poetry. As a musician, I see poems as cross-cut with unconscious and sometimes interfering images and phrases, or counterpoint rhythms that irrupt within our standard sense of the line. We make "sense," if that's the way to say it, just as often from making the opaque world speakable as from a self-conscious focus on our processes of speaking – whether those processes succeed or fail. Instead of being paralyzed into silence when process and product contradict each other, this is a moment when the act of composition, in poetry and music, sometimes can be its most exciting.

Baby June

Dice thrown behind a door.
        Lingering, the time comes,
                a presence, snow, there's no taxi.
                        Wedge like glass in the bus.

leave her in care of nurses and leave to go to work
days of cold Russian winter but we feel fine

Constellations, stories in the sky.
        The disappearing world is full
                of them. A mother is a city,
                        it foams at the mouth.

we both wanted a boy Marina feels well, baby girl, O.K.

The balcony by lamp light on green table.
        She is stout. The evening crackles.
                Russian custom, they make me
                    wait 10 days to see her.

Dear Marina: You and I are completely ready.
What do you need? Can you walk? Is June still red?

Shin Yu Pai

Bio: Shin Yu Pai is the author of *Sightings: Selected Works* [2000-2005] (1913 Press, 2007), *The Love Hotel Poems* (Press Lorentz, 2006), *Unnecessary Roughness* (xPress(ed), 2005), *Equivalence* (La Alameda Press, 2003), and *Ten Thousand Miles of Mountains and Rivers* (Third Ear Books, 1998). She received her MFA from the School of the Art Institute of Chicago where she studied writing and photography.

Poetic Statement:

Since my days at The School of the Art Institute of Chicago, my poetry has been heavily shaped by visual culture. As a grad student, my classroom was the Art Institute, where I spent many hours in the Tadao Ando gallery and the Joseph Cornell room, inspired by the artwork around me.

It seemed to me even then, that poetry is a dialogue – between poet and reader, between a poem and a work of art – centered largely around aesthetic sensibilities and individual process. As my work developed in complexity, this conversation began to take on a deeper social engagement, questioning visual culture and its power to influence and shape experience and perception.

The Love Hotel Poems are from a longer series of poems written in response to the work of documentary images of Japanese love hotels. Visual and narrative texts examine the role and culture of Japanese love hotels, blowing open the authoritarian narrative of the documentarian/social critic obsessed with Japan's sex fetishes who critiques the culture as outsider. The series looks at the culture and economy of love hotels, examining gender relations, the phenomena of cosplay, and behind-the-scenes workers in these artificial environments created to give pleasure and comfort.

The visual poems of my Nutritional Feed series were inspired by the work of New York painter David Lukowski, a colleague from my Boston days who labored alongside me in the same private healthcare setting—i.e. corporate America—while we both struggled to make time for our art. Mr. Lukowski's images are abstract narratives informed by the works of such artists as Jasper Johns and Jean-Michel Basquiat, drawing heavily upon popular culture and reflective of childhood and the American identity. My poetic texts engage the paintings in a dialogue concerning artistic process and treated the works as ekphrastic objects, tracking the process of eye, mind, and heart. Tupelo Press will release *Nutritional Feed* in 2007, in an edition that will publish the texts alongside the paintings.

← suck   squeeze   **B - A - N - G !**   b   l   o   w →

loosely sewn

      spaghetti western

story of   the good

                               & the ugly

          the bad

misdemeanors: possession

of firearm narcotic bootleg

now serving time

in the academy

(click here to apply)

Little Chapel Christmas, Nihonbashi

decked in plastic
trees a tangle

of electric lights
girls with the I.Q.s

of potted plants
mistletoe, ornament

pediment

pedophilic

fetishists

Xmas comes
365 days a year

something special slipped
into a stocking

what she wants –
a Burberry scarf,

or designer handbag
pleasure in a box of

knee socks and underwear

in this Nativity scene

Jesus the name
of just another john

How delightful everything is!
     or   ***Things that are dispensed from vending machines***

Hamburgers, hot dogs, and takoyaki.

Beer, sake, whiskey and milk.

Hooks and fishing bait.

D, C, and AA sized batteries.

Video games, vibrators, disposable cameras, and film.

Soiled schoolgirls' panties.

Toilet paper.

Omikuji*.

Live beetles. Rhinoceros and stag are especially popular for breeding or as pets.

Rice by the kilo.

Fresh vegetables picked this morning.

Breaded chicken, French fries, and fried sea bream.

*omikuji: strips of paper used for fortune telling sold at Shinto shrines

Dan Beachy-Quick

Bio: Dan Beachy-Quick teaches at the School of the Art Institute of Chicago. He is the author of three books of poetry: *North True South Bright, Spell,* and *Mulberry.* His essays and reviews appear variously. He is the recent recipient of a Lannan Foundation residency.

Poetic Statement:

    A poetic that precedes a poem privileges certainty of form over discovery in form. I feel myself devoted to the latter difficulty. I do not think a poem is lawless. I think, as with gravity, one writes and finds an entire physics operating within the world the poem opens. Except these laws latent inside the poem are not natural laws. The poem is not Quantum, not Newtonian, not Copernican, nor Ptolemaic, though every poem may indeed attempt not merely to map the universe, but claim a cosmogony it also, in its own self-utterance, replicates. The poem suffers the same fate as every inquiring explanation: it loses the very center from which it speaks. I can feel as I read, when I sit down with a great poem, an ordering cosmic force and a chaotic, disordering one. I can find in certain poems the struggle Robert Duncan speaks of finding in his own work: "wrestling with Form to liberate Form." The poem doesn't privilege cosmos over chaos. The poem has no other way back to chaos—that silent, fecund, nothingness which, by another name, we know as possibility—save through the paradoxical work of restricting the very motion it wishes to achieve. That limit is not a poetic, it is the work of the poem.

    For a poetic to be honest, in my mind, it must arise from the poem's work. As that work is never constant, never the same, always shifting, always a Heraclitean flux, the poetic that arises from it is never static. A poetic expresses the laws—both physical and metaphysical—the poem itself cannot express. The poem speaks according to these laws, not of them—just as I speak of gravity, not by mentioning the force, but by walking on the earth.

Of course, the next poem's work may reverse gravity. There is nothing a poem must not learn to betray.

I realize, reading this over, how abstract it is. I've learned, for better or worse, to expect such from myself. More strange, I realize how little I seem to be part of my own poetic. The poem feels to me more and more a kind of holy, anonymous work. A poem's relation to my own life, my own experience, parallels the same difficulty the poem has to its own formal limits. It just so happens that I am that limitation. As Thoreau writes, "I never dreamed of any enormity greater than I have committed. I never knew, and never shall know, a worse man than myself."

When I think over what I most wanted to say, I see how far astray thinking pulls me from purpose. I meant to speak of Henry David Thoreau. I wanted to quote at length Thoreau speaking of building his house, an activity as "of the same fitness . . . as in a bird's building its own nest." I hoped to speak about the work of considering a foundation before a cornice. And then, I meant to bring up a point I had never noticed until this most recent reading of *Walden*, that Thoreau built his house there by the power of his own hands because "it is one of the oldest scenes stamped on my memory." Thoreau returned to dig a foundation in the place of his first awareness. I wanted to suggest a poem is the very same work; we don't drop a word on a page so much as we put an inky edge into a blank field. For every word, or so it seems to me if I'm thinking clearly about it, has buried inside it the moment of our first awareness now stamped so indelibly into our memory. Except a word is inherited from millennia past, and the memory hidden within it is older than my experience of myself, or my experience of the world. There is first the moment of speaking when word and world collide into mutual co-meaning, when within the limits of my life I see something, and understand it for the first time. But that moment is but the surface to a more profound, more harrowing realization. That my experience of the world is deeper than my experience of myself, and a word brings with it a not-me more vast than the me who utters it. Every poem is written anonymously. A poem is a little house built on a blank foundation. The poet writes and expresses no more than a squatter's right on a page.

Difference in Triplicate

Watched the video of myself watching myself
On video   Here I am saying that's me
Saying here I am   Outside, the pixels so
Small each leaf I believe real   The birch-tree
With its paper-white bark that peels in reams
So paper figures doubt   Here I am watching
My absence watch me when one of me leaves
The room where paper-whites breathe the birch
Missing leaves all winter electrically blooms
Static on branch-tip grows mute   Echo announces
Her subject is doom   One of me returns as *Who
Are you?* grows convex along the curve of glass
Now empty in the other room   A word more known
In water drowns in air   A bee in the box
Blows dust beneath the buzz of wings on mute
I might watch the dust blow mute   I might
Balance the bee on my thumb   Now breath
Is gone   Might collect the carcass and call it my own
Here I am saying here it is with me in this room
On the bookshelf   Spine-broken Ovid stands
Next to the middle of my life   I woke in a dark wood
Somewhere near memory   I heard memory go mute
I wrote about the birch-tree on a line   I heard
Paper echo my mind   Now the screen is dark and one
Of me is not surprised   and one of me is blank
One of me says here I am   and one of me sees the hours
In manuscript   The dark letters widen in darkness
I have had many thoughts these months about the moon
But here there is no moon   Even when the moon is full
A book is about to close itself in the night closing itself
Or I saw a crow open and close its wings before a bulb
And never move   So another year passes
Backward through the year   These dark ideas
In ink in hand in pixel in blank this me saying to me
It's late   It's late   It's growing late

Cello Suite

The wasp in series the wasp
In cello notes the wasp wing
Nerved in echo with the drone
How late the light prisms
To lull and lend a bare slant
Curves the bowstring on the wall

On the wall the star divides white
In rainbow now the night will curl
Home into the wasp's dark flight
My headache shallow in silver bowl
Rings the wasp inside my ear
Curls the cello into our home

A red tone lashed to white is white
The bow must bend rosin so rose
Flowers in the silver bowl
Unpetal my ear in wasp's drone
To sing deny the cello sings
As light divides when prism sleeps

And dusk informs what glow to go
Low my headache rings Low
A last note stings below the nerve
Other times there is no pain   in series
The wasp in tune the wasp allowed
The cello string stops at evening's gasp

Maxine Chernoff

Bio: Maxine Chernoff is a professor and Chair of the Creative Writing program at San Francisco State University. With Paul Hoover, she edits the long-running literary journal *New American Writing*. She is the author of six books of fiction and eight books of poetry, most recently *Among the Names* (Apogee Press, 2005). Her work has appeared in many magazines including *Conjunctions, Zyzzyva, North American Review, Chicago Review, The Paris Review, Partisan Review, Sulfur, New Directions Annual, Denver Quarterly, Hambone, Slope,* and *Verse*. Her collection of stories, *Signs of Devotion,* was a *NYT Notable Book of 1993*. Both her novel *American Heaven* and her book of short stories, *Some of Her Friends That Year,* were finalists for the Bay Area Book Reviewers Award. Her novel *A Boy in Winter* is currently in production in Canada by an independent film company. With Paul Hoover, she has translated *The Selected Poems of Friedrich Hölderlin,* which will be published by Omnidawn Press in 2008. She has read her poetry in Liege, Belgium; Cambridge, England; Sydney, Australia; Berlin, Germany; Sao Paolo, Brazil; Glasgow, Scotland; Yunnan Province, China; and St. Petersburg, Russia. She lived in Chicago from 1952-1994.

Poetic Statement: Form and Function

According to Russian psychologist Alexander Luria, "With the help of language [humans] can deal with things they have not perceived even indirectly and with things which were part of the experience of older generations. This ability adds another dimension to the world of humans. . . .Animals have only one world, the world of objects and situations which can be perceived by the senses. Humans have a double world." In choosing verse or the prose poem, I am trying to accommodate my register of this double world to the form that best suits it. If I am thinking (or dreaming) of a world of objects that float in proximity to each other and create odd connections, as in the Frank O'Hara poem where two people pass each other and their "surgical implements lock for a day," then the best medium for that accidental conjunction is the prose poem. Many of my earliest prose poems written under the influence of masters such as Michaux and Cortazar work in that mode. It is as if the poem were conditional, "if X happens or should happen, then. . . " The prose poem gives me liberty to explore the accidental meetings, the space in which a fan speaks to an anonymous man who enters a room, or an artist designs a windmill of famous moustaches, or bridges of perishable items are erected to console man about mortality. I wanted a space in which I could explore the image and sustain its intensity with a deadpan speaker reporting on such events.

Later I moved to the prose poem to capture dialogue between speakers in a manner that respected the lengths and patterns of human utterance. These more recent prose poems, which are most often arguments between a man and a woman and have been adapted into a play by Mac Maginnes and staged at Small Press Traffic's Poets' Theater Festival in San Francisco, are terse and tense language duets that need the ragged borders and sentence patterns of prose. Were I to pay attention to line break or overly control rhythm, it would undermine the ebb and flow of the dialogue and truncate the human speech which strives to be realistic. These poems record social moments, often discord or misunderstanding and require an expansive form, which prose poems allow perhaps more easily than verse.

My other two more recent efforts have been in verse. The first is a series of poems based on "Gift Theory," which spans disciplines from literature to anthropology to philosophy to religion to economics and includes such important figures as Mauss, Godelier, Derrida, Emerson, and Irigaray, among others. My interest here was to extract a narrow, sinuous sonically-constructed poem from far longer non-poetic essays. It was a process of losing words or erasure that led to narrow poems that tumbled down the page.

My goal in extracting the essay's argument and in some poems providing a counter-argument is to contemplate all aspects of the gift as an economy and a vehicle for ethics.

The uneven vertical columns of words serve to emphasize individual phrases, juxtapose them to others, and maintain sonic connections and segues. Prose would not be adept at achieving the type of visual highlighting needed for words and phrases to be isolated and take on a proper weight, nor would it allow for the quickness with which I feel these arguments moving, almost as if they are a liquid medium being poured through a funnel.

In a few later poems of this sequence, I use several texts within one poem to create an argument of sources with each other. It is as if my former strategy in the dialogue poems has returned to pose a thesis and antithesis in the later poems of the gift texts. These fragments, then, become a long rope of connections and disputes with the line serving to insist on their forward movement.

I am again exploring similar possibilities in a book of poems that uses many diverse sources for sampling and borrowing from *Hamlet* to the news. One long poem in the collection locates sentences in individual texts and joins them together with anaphora using the female pronouns *she* or *her*. The poem explores "she" sentences in a variety of contexts from literary fiction to commercial fiction to prose essays in areas including economics, philosophy, art, and literary theory. I have found in beginning this project that there is a paucity of "she" sentences in most theoretical writing, so I have also given myself permission to change the arbitrary subject of a sentence from "he" to "she" when I so choose. Since I want the repeated word at the beginning of many sentences (such as the words "I saw," which open most lines of Ginsberg's *Howl)*, I am writing in extremely long lines that seem to break down the borders between poetry and prose.

In my case, then, the purpose, texture, speed, and sound of the writing seem to determine the form I choose, whether prose poem or verse. When I want more constraints, I will most often choose verse. When I want a dreamy exploration of objects and images or the ragged shapes of human speech, prose has served me better. Moreover, each project arrives with its own logic and constraints. I try to honor their inherent logic by choosing the form which best suits it.

121

Notes to Self

"Despite his moments of thralldom in. . . deepest Tunisia, Paul Klee refused to give up the vocabulary of children's art." –Roger Shattuck

1.
He knew the names of flowers,
the gem-like words for things—
unlike most of nature,
which, as it instructs,
ceases to entertain.

2.
Wegg's leg became a doll
before cyber-punks were born.
When they mapped the human genome
they found me lacking. This can
also be said of the real vs. virtual realm.

3.
A song of imperfection so lovely
as to defeat decadent aestheticism.
I saw it on TV. Karaoke.
People moving their lips, a girl
whispering inside a shadow-box.

4.
He pushed his stomach
out of his mouth to eat: must be
a starfish, our tour guide said.
Kristeva writes, "I expel myself.
I spit myself out."

5.
AM I GETTING IT RIGHT?
was scrawled on the bathroom wall.
Suggesting landscape and cloudscape,
as a sick man who imagines
the illness outside of himself.

6.

Anonymity was growing cold
when death technologies were invented.
She spoke of taking pains to
be a good host. But what do cyborgs eat?
she asked the Panel on Non-food Cuisine.

7.

"Don't worry. We won't let you die,"
culture said to anarchy.
Too few skeletons in the closet
to make things interesting. "Born
in Hoboken"is only half-epitaph.

8.

She thought she'd seen a ghost.
But disembodiment is a technological
fantasy, meant to signify transcendence
of materiality. No syntax
for the concept of memory vs. Memorex.

9.

He said of the abdominal cavity:
"Such a primitive place. One expects
to find paintings of buffalo on the wall."
Inside the gallery was another gallery.
Inside that a sanctuary.

10.

I've never met a utopia I didn't like.
Simulated war and simulated pain.
 "This is not a pipe" written in mind or eye.
Simulated love on the Simulator Channel.
A home inside the neutral gleam.

Have You a Daughter?

1.

to get cold feet

    to make no headway

to be on tenderhooks

    (my eyes are wide)

to eat nettles

    stinging nettles

to embroider flowers

    to take one's heart out

2.

the crimes

    were linguistic

    reduced to

a novel

    the lowest form of humor

no puns intended

3.

the method Socratic

     (reality of the word)

"Let her
     not walk in the sun"

4.

When she wakes

     from her nap,

she knows all her sins

     can't be forgiven

5.

A melancholy awareness

     drives her to the shore

     where an impossible pair

(mermaid and whale)

     were last seen

6.

faithful to the text

        as a nun or priest

whose small offering

        is worthy of omniscience

          (worthy of God)

but only in the text—

7.

        in life she was scattered

she couldn't see her hand

        in front of his face

her face erased

        by fog and intention

8.

you blaspheme she said

        to the lilies and orchids

when like a season

        (far-fetched in excess)

they bloomed in the mirror

and also the world

9.

radiant

and strange

an element of reason

(no harm intended)

for her subjectivity

to calculate a reason

(winter death/spring resurrection)

a world

like an orchid

or lily

no harm in a vase

the stinging nettles

10.

your poor and erring breast

since I cannot remember

all the deaths

(the devil's in the details)

and you

made to want

to scarify

to mark

as if to heal

the beauty before us

arriving as it did

11.

I have no daughter

he said in the play

yet if she existed

he wouldn't deny

the hyperbole

or song

128

Kerri Sonnenberg

Bio: A Chicagolander since the age of 1, Kerri Sonnenberg is the author of *The Mudra* (Litmus Press, 2004). From 2002 to 2004 she published *Conundrum*, a journal of poetry and cross-genre writing. In 2003 she founded The Discrete Reading Series with Jesse Seldess. She has taught poetry workshops to children and adults through programs with The Poetry Center, The Chicago Public Library, and Woodland Pattern Book Center. *Practical Art Criticism* first appeared as a chapbook published by Milwaukee's Bronze Skull Eights Press in 2004.

Poetic Statement:
At the beginning of a long summer, a friend left a book on my living room table called *Practical Art Criticism*. It was a thin paperback scarcely 150 pages with an abrasively stark white cover and black text. It glared at me every day as life was lived around it, a life, as any life, not separate from art itself. Both are experience, making and being made by/amid the wily ephemera of the American semiosphere, culled and gussied up by sensual experience and held in some recess of the mind for further study. I never read the parent book, but wrote this brief tract to it, and for a renegotiation of language and art in a time of truthiness and reality television.

Practical Art Criticism

if light only inherited her doing
and invention from the courage of their common features
        betters passengers
we are free to answer "yes"
a plank to the visual facts resting in television

or architecture once it's believed: the premises
sounds like evasion at sea
        metabolism, devotion
in defensive shapes
orange or an orange
        belongs to purpose, persuasion

for each object
a ballpark we speak
unlike radiant disuse

evened memories patina to
physical
        given ceremony
a suit beside not spring

full of voices coincides machinery
          the artist intrinsic to
bells sufficiencies
toward the ground whether
an instrument is looking
"like it is" or is over a formal square
doing the looking

at the same tine also has the ability
to eat sleep staccato viewers' remove
but that blood fruit
          makeover alchemical
leads through through

which is to say "the goods" analogous
lived outside traffic jams, burst events
playing ghost with
          systems, what cure
is her song lowering scythe

with a lens, restore
without the judges, diffuse,
with judgment shiv
to make meaning clear
as a possible object, late in its season
sees the script

these same words plus a warning form
an audience, with orders
for restive images light a rapport

death undergirds
"meaning" with criteria for "work"

splinters legitimately the floating device

Jesse Seldess

Bio: Jesse Seldess recently relocated from Chicago to Berlin to Karlsruhe. In Chicago, he co-curated The Discrete Reading and Performance Series with Kerri Sonnenberg. In Berlin, he organizes The Floating Series of exhibitions and events with Leonie Weber as well as continues to edit *Antennae*, a journal of experimental writing, music, and performance. Chapbooks of his poems have been published by Answer Tag Home Press, Bronze Skull Press, and the Chicago Poetry Project, and his first full-length book of poems, *Who Opens*, appeared on Kenning Editions early in 2006.

Poetic Statement:
I approach dynamics or environments or circumstances and try to register and move through the relational fullness of instances, the simultaneity of present/encountered and speculative/ empathetic life, working through that materialistically, in time and sound, permuting language, beginning, halting, combining, extending directions. "In Contact" developed from my time with seniors afflicted with Alzheimer's or dementia resulting from other conditions.

from *In Contact*

End

And end

By past will

Hand talking
By past will

Tend

And talking by

And walking by

By fast will

Hand

Finding view

Or you by talking

For you by talking

Close up

Hand talking by

With incompletely
Finding view

To be
Close up

Or face

In talking

To be close up

By talking

To be close
Up by talking

Up by face

By you talking

In you by talking

By you

And talking by

And walking by

And in face

Finding view
To be close

And face filled

With incompletely
Finding view

To be close
Or face

For here instance

To be close
For here face

To stretch over
Or close

Or face

To be close
Or sketched over
Or face

To be close
Or sketched
Or face

To be sketch over
Or close
Or face

To be sketched
Over face

In contact
To be close
Or face

To be close

In contact
Stretched over
Or face

Finding view

From that instance
Finding view

For that instant

Or face

To be
Stretched

Finding view

sketched
In that instance

Or face

To be close

Near that mouth
From here instance

Finding view
In that mouth

With incompletely
Finding view
From here
In that

Or face

With incompletely

Finding view
From here

Audible

To be close

Finding view audible
In here

With incompletely
Finding
View audible

Paul Hoover

Bio: Paul Hoover's most recent books are *Edge and Fold* (Apogee Press, 2006), *Poems in Spanish* (Omnidawn, 2005), *Winter Mirror* (Flood Editions, 2002), *Rehearsal in Black* (Salt Publications, 2001), *Totem and Shadow: New & Selected Poems* (Talisman House, 1999), *Viridian* (University of Georgia Press, 1997), and *The Novel: A Poem* (New Directions, 1990). He is editor of the anthology *Postmodern American Poetry* (W. W. Norton, 1994) and, with Maxine Chernoff, the annual literary magazine *New American Writing*. His collection of literary essays, *Fables of Representation*, was published by University of Michigan Press in 2004. He has also published a novel, *Saigon, Illinois* (Vintage Contemporaries). In 2002, he won the Jerome J. Shestack Award for the best poems to appear in *American Poetry Review* that year. A long-time Chicago resident, he is Professor of Creative Writing at San Francisco State University.

Poetic Statement:

I'm more or less a Romantic ironist. Delineated by Schlegel, Novalis, and Schelling around 1797, Romantic irony emerged from the dialectic between relativism and the absolute. Sometimes called "indeterminacy," this position blends doubt and belief, rejects certainty, and actively seeks negotiation with the flawed and half-veiled. Much of which we take to be Modernism and Postmodernism, especially the famous insufficiency of word to world, derives from such a concept. Everything is contingent, ironic, and pluralistic, but it is also serious and forceful. The language poets follow the line passing back through Objectivism, Pound and Stein, Materialism, and Pragmatism. They are suspicious of lyricism as collaborating with the metaphysical. I follow the line back through the New York School, Wallace Stevens, German Romanticism and Idealism. Such poets enjoy the game of representation played by the copy and the model. But without a sense of humor, such thinking descends into mysticism.

142

Poetics

I have no objectives, no system, no tendency, and no plan.
I have no speech, no tongue, no memory, and no realm.
Because nothing matters, I am consistent, committed, and excited.
I prefer the definite, the bounded, the repressed and the weak.
Not objectivity but neutrality of being.
Not spontaneity but panic.
For only seeing believes and only the body thinks.
For success is common to those who fail.
For the world's beauty is fading because the world is fading.
For the best narrative is always oblique.
For thought only thinks it thinks—all has been foretold.
For without cruelty, there would be no beauty.
For kindness is always a little bit tragic.
For the mind's progress is zigzag and stabs at every tree.
For the best art makes things disappear.

Eating Ideas

If they went beyond the husk,
the seed lay gleaming.

If they went beyond the flesh,
the bone lay pale.

They were eating the dialectic
and the marrow of difference.

They consumed abhorrence
and something Duns Scotus said.

They went beyond desire,
past "qualitative forms,"

a "tactics of resistance,"
and radical grammar.

They were eating ideas.
Space unfurled around them.

Time let down its gown.
Dominant systems of sense-making

had nothing left to say
but said it now and then.

Nothing was left to love,
but much could be declared:

abandonment of history,
the future passing away.

They were hungry for a moment,
but time would not comply.

They had eaten their ideas,
and dessert was still to come—

some kind of essence
with existence in its wings.

The Lower Depths

A tiger means bamboo.
Bamboo means a sparrow.
A sparrow means music,

And music means a soul.
Soul means a heart,
and heart means a body

weeping in the street.
The street means dust,
and dust means traffic.

The world means itself
in silence and disquiet.
Disquiet means science,

and beauty means
practice, when the mind
makes its mess and

puts it back in order.
Order means mistakes;
pleasure means wisdom;

wisdom means seeing.
To see is to know,
and knowing means mercy.

Mercy means a mountain.
Snow means companion.
Apple means shadow,

shadow on the tree.
Nothingness says nothing.
It's something

makes our sounds.
O taste and see,
dark upon the harp.

A harp means distance.
Distance leads to pity.
A rock leads to water.

Water finds two rivers.
A river goes home,
and home means fate,

where history takes
vacations, where they
have to let it in.

Written

1

There was a written stone
In the unwritten river,
And written rain was falling
Over the written town.
Nothing written today
But tomorrow I'll be written
As I sit in my room unwriting.
This was already written
When I found it sitting here.
It never quite escapes
What it was meant to be,
A suicide note half written
Before the act half-done.

2

Nothing isn't empty.
It fills a room so completely
It spills into the street,
Which of course looks empty
Because nothing is there.
Nothing is filled with nothing,
Everything comes from nothing.
Something, poor something,
Stands vacant at the door.
A rose opens and opens
Until its petals fall.
Then it seems vacant,

Like a room with one chair.
Beauty is always vacant.
We know an object best
When it starts to disappear.
Words are here but nothing,
Meaningful sounds passing
Then nothing but pleasure.
Light and space are something
Passing through the trees.
A cry is heard in the distance.
Remembered by your senses,
It is something briefly
And then present absence.

3

A background seems like nothing
Until a figure emerges, from what
Seems the beginning.
          There is no beginning.
Along with its nothing,
Something always comes before,
Receding here, approaching there.
Only you remain to bring it
Back from somewhere—
That shade of blue in the hallway,
The black depths of water.
Yellow fires, gray earth, and green
Of wheat are something: actors
Without equal, cock crowing town.

4

Everything nature says
Is ancient, careless, and cruel,
But it has no concept of nothing.
It leans against a sunlit wall,
Projecting casually something.
A mirror out of doors
Catches our eye because
Our eyes are in it, because
It seems to eye us as part

Of its nature shining.
Someone put it there
To be twice something.
The overlord language resides
There, too: a stain, nerve knot,
With its incessant naming.
It comes into being, breathes,
Then goes back out again.
"What was that?" we ask.
"Did you hear something?"
"It was nothing," says the cook.
"A ghost," insists the chaplain.
"It was dinner," says the hen,
So philosophical lately,
And always about one thing.

Michelle Taransky

Bio: Michelle Taransky is from South Jersey and was educated at The University of Chicago. Taransky's poems appear in *La Petite Zine, DIAGRAM, 88: A Journal of Contemporary American Poetry, canwehaveourballback?,* and *Drunken Boat.*

Poetic Statement:

These poems are from a series about a family whose farm burns down and then runs a bank on the same site. The project performs—again and again—acts of a similar violence on perceptions.

Barn Burner, If

What lays down here
Does not call

For the plan
Its facts of

Carve and split some-
Thing rare to hillocks like

Frocks do
Want those unwed

Stories of fault

Lines the barn was
Plotted on

Hold fawns if
Slatted if elder spare
All able bodied for
A final spot

In the clearing only
If it wasn't bough

But corner of petite
Angle the leave

's curling margins
Coop and pen

No stall if
Ovate then

. . . Blaze the
Bricks will

I don't stop for

The yearling

Loses touch

Bank Branch

State of fall
I mean fall
Leaves

Saying a season
Is not an only answer
Probability of rotting

That permits
Door-keeper as well
As the door he left

A teller never their
Worries about

The red horse &
Confession
Folded into threshold

Glass statement
Promising *I won't see you anymore*
A likeness

Here fixing causes that dream
To be about a bank

A blood-like retreat
From root
For trust

Going to war
Changing brother is
Going to get there

Robert Archambeau

Bio: Robert Archambeau's books include *Word Play Place* (Ohio/Swallow), *Vectors: New Poetics* (Samizdat), *Home and Variations* (Salt) and *Laureates and Heretics* (Notre Dame). He's a critic as well as a poet, and teaches at Lake Forest College. Formerly the editor of *Samizdat*, he now co-directs the &NOW Festival of Innovative Art and Writing. Born in Rhode Island in 1968, he grew up in Canada, and he vividly remembers his parents considering, then rejecting, the idea of putting an "America: Love it or Leave it" bumper sticker next to their Manitoba license plates. He has taught at Lund University in Sweden, but has called Chicago home for a decade or more.

Poetic Statement:

I seem to return again and again to two main themes. For lack of better terms, let's call them "culture and displacement" and "aesthetics in a world of power." I suppose my somewhat peripatetic upbringing has something to do with the first theme: my family was always shuffling around between two countries, and my father, an artist, was very concerned with the idea of tradition in art. So I became interested in the movement of cultural traditions, and the idea of people inventing themselves out of their place, their reading, their music, and the like. Ideas of this kind crop up in "Home and Variations" and, in slightly different form, in "Two Short Films...". As for the other theme, I suppose it comes from being deeply committed to — no, the better phrase would be *in love with* — aesthetic expression, but at the same time wondering just what kind of place it has in a world of power, brutality, and real consequences. I suppose "Poem for a War Poet, Poem for a War" is a poem in this vein.

By way of explaining why I work as a critic as well as a poet, I can only really say this: things seem to come to me first as poetry, and later as prose. The "culture and displacement" theme gets followed up on in my new critical book, *Laureates and Heretics*, and

153

the "aesthetics in the world of power" business has me excited about working on new book of criticism too.

Of course anything I say about my own habitual themes is as suspect as anyone's self-representation. No one has much objectivity regarding their own work. Sometimes it takes comments by a friend or a critic to shake you up and show you other sides to what you've been doing: I remember reading a review of *Home and Variations* that claimed the book was all about fathers, origins, and lost innocence. After a few minutes of incredulity, I was entirely convinced. And a little alarmed that I hadn't noticed those things before. I mean, you think you know yourself. . . .

Anyway. Perhaps a better way of making a statement about my work would be to quote an artist I admire, who has been a mentor to me in more ways than you'd imagine: "I get up in the morning, have a good cup of coffee, a bit of breakfast and go to work. In the studio as in my life I expect nothing but hope for the best."

Poem for a War Poet, Poem for a War

1.

The lines inked on the map are railways and roads.
The lines on the roads are refugees, and moving.
The lines inked on the page are a poem, your poem.
> *While you are singing, who will carry your burden?*

The lines on the page are a poem, words
that move toward the refugees, their tattered world
of hurt and proper names, their lost, their staggering.
> *While you are singing, while you are singing.*

The lines are helpless in this time of war. They survive,
if they are a poem, in valleys of their saying, they survive
and reach for valleys where bodies cough, bleed or stumble blind.

They survive while you are singing,
        While you are singing.

2.

The lines on the roads are refugees,
Their paths are marked with ink, charted
on a General's table. Your lines are a poem.
        While you are singing, who will carry your burden?

A woman bends beneath her load, a young man stutters in his fear,
A guard at the valley's border lets them through,
or not. Your lines are a poem.
        Who will carry your burden?

Home and Variations

Some stay in one place.
Others move. Still others move
from place to place, staying
for a while. But some
stay in one. And if they think of this,
they call it "home." Stop.
And if those who stay in one place
and know it are at home, others, moving, or
moving place to place to stay
and move, are not.
And if they know it, know
they're not at home. Stop.
And if they stayed in one place and moved on
and if they know it, then they know that
when they hadn't moved, they were at home.
Whether they knew it. Whether they not.
Stop.
And if they left and know they left
they feel a lack.

And others stay in one place. And if
they stay and the place won't stay as
the place they knew was the place that's "home" they feel
a lack. Stop. And this tells.
And some who feel a lack will fill
the lack they feel. Stop. And my father
played the phonograph. Played sea chanteys,
played Hank Snow. Played them till my mother,
or went and played them till they stopped. Stop. Played
at being with the sailors, played at being
with Hank Snow. Played at doing what
they did, which wasn't play. Stop. If work
was what men did with hands and tools
on farm and sea and if my father's father worked
with hands and tools but didn't sing. Would the
singing of the sailors would the singing of Hank Snow
be singing so my father he could play at
being home. Stop. And if his son who moved, and
moved from place to place. Whether he wanted.
Whether he not. If he thought of father thinking father
thinking work and farm and home would
the thinking take him farther would the thinking take him home.

Two Short Films
on the translation of the European imagination to America

… what we feel of sorrow and despair
From ruin and from change, and all the grief
The passing shews of being leave behind,
Appeared an idle dream ….
    Wordsworth, The Prelude

Up to now literature has exalted a pensive immobility, ecstasy, and sleep.
We intend to exalt aggressive action, a feverish insomnia …
   Marinneti, Futurist Manifesto

1. Wordsworth at the Cuyahoga's Mouth, 1796-1996

In newsreel stock, in jumpy monochrome
You mount the windy bluff, glance back and turn
To face the valley. Far below, white water foams

Birds cry, and black waves peel from slabs of rock,
Back down to the great lake's boom and suck.
You stand, a silhouette, black coat and stick.

The film moves quickly now – clouds fly and light's
A flickered blur of days and nights. You wait,
The still point of a world that's turned to haste.

You wait, and plowed lines break the dark earth's crust –
The valley peopled now – and frontier huts
Crop up each harvest time. A rail line thrusts

On past that limestone ridge, with quick faint wraiths
That, caught in a frame that stutters through the gate,
Are horses, wagons, wide-backed men. You wait,

Brick chimneys frame the screen and black smoke swells,
A furnace-city churns its molten steel –
And one quick night's a flash: city plays hell.

And you, above this growth and flux and ruin,
Does your sleepwalker-muse fetch Whitman songs
Great port, great ore-port, great handler of iron –

Or bring *an image of tranquility*
So calm and still, a green dream's tapestry
Of soft grass overgrowing history?

I can't expect an answer: You stand, there,
And breathe the flickered light of setting suns, the living air.

2. *Marinneti at Union Station, Chicago*

Arrived, the locomotive paws the track,
deep-chested, bellowing

(we gather, from this silent reel);
its steam-plumes jet in cavern air

beneath the city. And, arrived –
in the city of railyards,

apparatus, of stokers groping blackened
through the mill-fire's angry blast,

the city of shipping, chemical manufacture,
stockyards blazed with electric moons – you,

mounting the platform, gestures broad,
erratic, oratorical.

Saying (we barely see, white letters
over faded stock) *Hold no ideal mistress high,*

her form divine rising to touch clouds;
saying *All must be swept aside,*

to express our whirling life of steel, of pride,
of fever and exalted speed;

saying, in that rush of sailors, workmen,
quick-eyed thieves, *death to Ciceroni, antiquarians. . .*

Mechanic-limbed and darting, the crowd
won't pause to hear you, and I

wonder, do you dream of Venice,
soft, past-loving, shocked

in all her statuary, when you declared
The fist dawn in now, and explosive breath?

You, erratic, oratorical, the last frame
fading on your words, *our bodies die for speed*

for movement and for darting light.

Bill Marsh

Bio: Bill Marsh was born in Chicago, where he attended St. Barnabas grade school until the age of ten. A series of family moves brought him to a small town in northern Virginia overlooking the Potomac River. It was here that Bill started imitating dead poets. Later, after earning degrees in English, Creative Writing, and Communication, Bill resettled in the town of Ottawa, Illinois, where, according to local legend, "Lincoln's voice was first heard." Bill also spends time in New York City, where he co-directs Factory School, a learning and production collective engaged in action research, publishing, media display, and community service.

Poetic Statement

All writing is plagiarism except where it pretends to be something else, and these poems are no exception. They are representative, then, of what I like to imagine are the limits of poetic structure and, perhaps, poetic imagination itself. The trick to reading them is to place them one over the other, with the "template" on the bottom, and then to hold them up to a bright artificial light, such as a CRT computer screen or a TV tuned to Channel One. Poems tend to overwrite their own production, their own genesis, in other words. Design, finally, is key—an argument I make in a poem not included here. Otherwise, I've learned that writing poetry is like refereeing an Epicurean orgy: all sensation, judged at a comfortable distance.

N. RIMES

[template]

evo cat

eva sum

a e i o (you)

evo sum

eva cat

2 0 _ 0 2

resume?

sure

a muse

a ruse?

mum

reuse

evo a

eva o

e i e i (thru)

N. 1

reason moot

motive coarse

manic riven muse

motive moot

reason coarse

music must amuse

acute?

carve

a tome

a mute?

note

of some

reason rime

motive mire

nervous ammo ruse

N. 2

romance mort

eros strum

ocean serum note

romance strum

eros mort

craven rose omit

ascent?

trace

a mouse

a voice?

cute

and moist

romance cure

eros come

restive oeuvre out

N. 3

covet tao

costume air

service novice rain

covet air

costume tao

cantor never vain

convince?

crust

marine

avert?

moon

unseen

covet smart

costume art

monic to insane

Larry Sawyer

Bio: Larry Sawyer mines diverse poetic ground and calls it methodology. He's taken cues from many schools but credits the Latin American poets, especially Vallejo, as spiritual ancestors. His poetry and critical reviews have been published in periodicals including *MiPOesias, Court Green, Jacket, the Prague Literary Review, Hunger, Skanky Possum, Moria, Arson,Range, Exquisite Corpse, Big Bridge, Skidrow Penthouse, the Tiny*, and elsewhere. He edits www.milkmag.org (since 1997) and also curates the reading series at Myopic Books in the Wicker Park neighborhood of Chicago.

Poetics Statement:
　　　Language is an obstruction to communication, it doesn't facilitate communication. Poetry, as I see it, isn't an attempt at communication. But in the rivulets of language, poetry is. A poem that is effective on many levels plays off of readers' expectations. In contemporary society anyone reading poetry on a regular basis probably has more than a passing interest in the subject. Not being a formalist, I primarily write poems that are open in form rather than closed. Disjointed syntax, rough associations, bizarre imagery, humor, assonance, enjambment, and metaphor raise the attention level and provide necessary momentum. Fresh understanding of the banal may arise from seemingly trivial juxtapositions in poems among seemingly disparate elements. Poetry should reawaken or reintroduce the reader to experience but not in any didactic sense. Effective poems are objects that enact rather than describe, so that is the ultimate goal of whatever methodology to which I ascribe. High, middle, and low levels of diction are all fair game when I'm writing. I'm never attempting to "say" anything, although memory plays a role in my modus operandi. I'm more concerned with the expressionist quality of poems on the image level versus the sentence level. On one end of the spectrum poets are the "babblers of ecstasy" but on the other end of the spectrum poets really are metaphysicians of undiscovered realms who map the absolute.

Me Tronome

I'd like to make a home in your beautiful neck
your violin neck plays beautiful concertos
I strain my ears as high as the treetops

so that I may hear them
there is a staircase in my heart
the black insect of midnight is calling us
we will crush
empires of midnights beneath our poor boots
our boots shaped like tired waves
upright sleepwalking dreams
charming excuses marching like regiments
at war with our best intentions
amateur day rises majestically
limpid and green
spring pigeons speak
forgotten languages and illustrate
frozen memories from a lost
cousin's blonde nightmare.

Poets

Wear the blue sweater of memory.
The days ahead won't be easy.

Make a world noise, because
the future is already here.

Advertising turned us into mosquitoes.

Galaxies in the distance still sculpt
the gism of the void.

BLUNT EDGE

for Ted Joans

*

I wanted to give you a weapon
of onyx and saffron
implement it in the dark nights
when all alone among bad poets
while sipping cumulonimbus
and puffing stratosphere
poetry is better than anything else
its death has been pronounced repeatedly
but they'll never really nail it down
it is a cocaine rose
a rubble hurricane
balloon eyes above actual flags
flapping along infinity
with our tongues we put on the finishing touches.

Lina ramona Vitkauskas

Bio: Lina ramona Vitkauskas is sick of symmetry. Her mother forced her to lay down where a priest made a hole in her head and took out the stone of madness. She is a Lithuanian-American poet and short fiction writer, born of Lithuanian parents from Germany and Brazil. She came from the East coast before coming to live in a south-side Chicago Lithuanian neighborhood. She is author of the book *THE RANGE OF YOUR AMAZING NOTHING* (Ravenna Press, 2007) and the chapbooks *Failed Star Spawns Planet/Star* (dancing girl press, 2006) and *Shooting Dead Films with Poets* (Fractal Edge Press, 2004). She has contributed a preface to the previously translated French fiction novella by author Denis Emorine titled, *A Step Inside* (Foothills Publishing, 2006). She has an M.A. in Creative Writing from Wright State University and is the co-editor of *milk magazine* (www.milkmag.org,1999-present) and contributing Lithuanian editor for *UniVerse, A United Nations of Poetry* (www.universeofpoetry.org).

Recent and forthcoming publications include *Another Chicago Magazine, Aufgabe, The Prague Literary Review, Van Gogh's Ear* (Paris), *Echolocation* (University of Toronto), *Arabesques* (Algeria), *Paper Tiger* (Australia), *The Chicago Review, Unpleasant Event Schedule, La Petite Zine, The Mississippi Review, The Wisconsin Review, Lituanus* (Lithuanian Quarterly Journal), and *In Posse Review Multi-Ethnic Anthology* (Ilya Kaminsky, editor). She won an Honorable Mention for *STORY Magazine's Carson McCullers Award* (1999) and was a semi-finalist in the *Cleveland State University Open Poetry Series* (2002). She has read all over Chicago, including at *The Balzekas Museum Of Lithuanian Culture, Myopic Books, Around the Coyote Arts Festival,* and *Woman Made Gallery,* where she will be a curator of a poetry series in fall of 2007.

Poetic Statement:
> "You cease to exist when you say, 'that's what I am'."
> —Alejandro Jodorowsky

Intention

blood is blood
a girl is temporary
small & yellow
pasteurized & nyloned
listen
you are not
my intention

day skin statistics
exhaling flint & grammar
you really
shouldn't
with
reality
but you do

the body stung numb
seed heart isotopes
the women above you
construct lowercase syntax

seem sallow & rusted
truncated & beligerent
tangled in marsh membranes
vacant diseases
used

to be
a censor
and now
a lopped, bleeding birch
the shoes of any man in the womb
already a bitter catapult

How Your Canary Tethers

plum knees,
door jambs undone
for now his reach as tiring as

the circle of circadian death,
the geometry of homonym
or as blotto breath through a

pale understudy of Minsk.
She has been Eros, his
chambermaid this long,

an even cog and spoke,
trusty gale and centerpiece,
rubicund permafrost,

misty delinquent damsel.
How he has calibrated woman
with the livered beak,

one that could not
be whet once more! How
each filigree innuendo

a phonograph torte
misguided lips a tortoise
she has hared anonymously.

Cecilia Pinto

Bio: Having lived in the mid-west for many years, Cecilia Pinto recalls with pleasure her childhood in New Jersey and post-college life in New York City. She thinks of herself as part prairie, part Jersey. She live happily in Chicago with her husband and sons.

Poetic Statement:

I believe in the breath. The words come to me as sound before they are words. I love a long line but always strive for brevity. I am always conscious of melody. I believe the poet is obligated to generosity towards the reader whatever that means to the poet. I believe in explanation but also in subterfuge. If I thought you needed to know more, I would tell you.

Fido

Our hero never came through the door without something in his hands; some thing in a wrinkled, brown paper bag, something loosely wrapped in crinkling plastic. A sturdy, paper shopping bag with handles, the thing inside sliding heavily back and forth; slump, slump.

Sometimes the thing is hidden inside his jacket or shoved in his back pocket. Once or twice in a bucket, or a jar, of pickles, or a jar of something else.

I want to say that once he pulled open his jacket and a canary yellow bird blew out and fluttered onto the head of the youngest child. A child absorbed in mashed banana or cookie or noodles with a little broth. The bird pecked, pulled a strand from the boy's own yellow thicket of hair, pulled a coin, a jewel, a golden bee.

But that would be a fairy tale and this is not that. Not a fantasy. Do not look for a moral, do not wait for the end expecting surprise or resolution, there may not be one. I'm warning you.

A little velvet box, a part from a train, seven balloons, tangerines in a wooden crate with the orange word Mandarin glowing on the side above a junk that sails under the black and blue eyed moon, (take a breath) a handful of straws.

Each evening he presents his package, his parcel, his bundle, his gift to the family. His wife, his mother, the children. Not everything was needed. Or wanted. Or desired. But it was given. Were they delighted? I don't know. Maybe it got routine, maybe they didn't know where to put everything, maybe, when he wasn't looking, they threw things out, but maybe not.

Things pile up. This on top of that in the laundry basket. Nothing can be found in the desk drawer when needed or at the bottom of the bag, but there it is anyway. And every day there is something new to put on top of something else, or in it or, underneath it. It becomes a game, like rock, paper, scissors. It becomes a life.

Mornings he left the house. After his breakfast of bread with butter and sugar dipped in milky coffee. He wiped his hands on a dish towel; it said Tuesday, it said Thursday. He kissed his wife.

See him walking down the cobblestone street with the humpty houses? See him hanging gray and pallid, long on a rung of subway train? No? See him talking to the deer? He could be, he could be feeding deer. That could be his job. The deers' ears twitch when they hear something. Their noses are mushroom velvet and good witch black.

Stop.
Find the youngest child you know who can speak and pass your fingertips over their shoulder and down their arm. This might be what it feels like to touch the deer. This might be a map you can trust.

The deer are across the meadow in the woods. There are Cornflowers, there are Indian Paint-Brushes, there are Buttercups and Queen Anne's Lace. There is Clover. I have not chosen arbitrarily. I am thinking of a specific meadow, one from my childhood, you should look at pictures if you have to.
Every day he walks across the meadow. On his back is an old canvas knapsack with two sandwiches wrapped in waxed paper and a thermos of something to drink. And maybe an apple, he should eat some fruit, something with seeds and juice.
Just now, as I take a breath, I discover I love him. It is the little things; the way the coffee soaks the bread, the knife with the bone handle he carries to cut the fruit, his pork pie hat which I have just given him. I tried different hats, that one looked the best. He shoves it on his head, surprised to find it there. He is just what I like; lean and a little dirty. I wish he were chocolate.

(I would like to say there is a dog with him, but there is not. There is no dog because it would be too much. You would begin to see the main character only in a certain way, and I don't want that. You are probably already making associations. However, just for a moment; see the dog? He's a herd dog, black and white and brown. He smiles as he nips at the rumps of his charges, his duty gives him pleasure. Does your duty give you pleasure?)

Truthfully, my hero only feeds the deer because they appear here and what else could he do but care for them? Well, I know he could do other things, but he's mine, so he is kind to animals.

173

He is really a chimney sweep. He carries a pig. Do you know this story? It is German, I think, or Austrian or Viennese. I once had a postcard that said about it. Should you happen to see a chimney sweep carrying a pig at the beginning of the year it is a sign of good luck. Somewhere in Europe people exchange cards to make this so, to make it so they see this man.

This impossibility.

What would it be like to see him or, to be him? The pink pig grunting under an arm, you or me covered in soot, and everyone happy to see you or me, everyone, always.

For whom is this intended?
To whom am I indebted?

I would like to offer you slices of an orange, a deer's antler, hot chocolate delicious in a beautiful mug. Would you like a crisp, green pickle or the feather from a yellow bird? I could give you these things. I know where to get them. I know this guy. He's always got something up his sleeve, in his pocket, under his hat. The hat that I gave him when I made him up; for luck, as a present, as the best I have to offer today. Tomorrow I will bring you something else.

Johanny Vázquez Paz

Bio: Johanny Vázquez Paz was born and raised in San Juan, Puerto Rico. She holds a Bachelor of Arts in Sociology from Indiana State University and an M. A. in Hispanic Studies from the University of Illinois at Chicago. She is the co-editor of the anthology *Between the Heart and the Land / Entre el corazón y la tierra: Latina Poets in the Midwest* published by MARCH/Abrazo Press. Her poems have been included in many journals and anthologies, including the new compilation *Poetas sin tregua* of Puerto Rican poets from the 80's generation. She presently teaches Spanish at Harold Washington College.

Poetic Statement:

I write *en español,* the only way I can express myself. Then I translate what I write, in order for others to understand. There are two poets in me: the one that follows the drum beat of the Nuyorican, Chicano, US-Latino poets with their social oriented, anti-discrimination power tool poetry; and the other one, born in the island of Puerto Rico, more lyrical, poetic, full of imagery, academic, intense, mature; because in Latin America poetry is a matter of life and death.

The poem "Our Revolution" is from *Streetwise Poems/Poemas callejeros* (Mayapple Press, February, 2007) a collection of urban poems that explores the impact of moving from the Caribbean to the Windy City.

Our Revolution

Since they don't let us have a revolution,
since communism went out of style
and they keep us informed every day
of Fidel's mistakes.

Since there are no longer wars for noble causes
and they have forgotten about defending the rights
of the poor, of women and children.

Since they devoted themselves to stealing crumbs
to fatten bank accounts in Switzerland,
and they gave orders to kill a friend, an enemy,
a neighbor or relative,
for little reason and much egoism.

Since people don't have control of anything
because it's easy to falsify ballots,
then,
let's close the door and jump into bed
like friendly enemies.

Many battles have been won in bed
with very little blood spilled,
and the equality of the sexes has been declared
and, in most of the cases studied, the superiority of women...

and I will be Bolívar
        and you all of America completely surrendered to me,
and you will be Che and I Bolivia's jungle healing your wounds,
and I will be Lolita Lebrón
        and you Albizu hand in hand for the same cause,
and you will be Pancho Villa
        and I Zapata north and south with no divisions,
and I will be Sandino and you Allende without a world power
that could silence us.

Since they don't let us dream with Utopia,
then,

bury your sword in me so I will yell for the two of us:
Freedom!

Ela Kotkowska

Bio: Born in Poznań , Poland , Ela Kotkowska resides in Chicago. Her translations from Polish and French appeared in the *Poetry Magazine* and *Chicago Review*, and her original work in *Chicago Review, Moria, Seven Corners*. A chapbook *Nom de Plume* was published by Yen Agat Press, 2004 & 2005. She is now writing her dissertation on René Char at Northwestern University .

Poetic Statement:
The winter of 2005-2006 was punctuated with daily walks along the lake's shore, mostly between Albion and Farwell. Because I dislike sun bathing, the beach had always little appeal. And because I can't swim, the open waters have always been inaccessible. The edge was what caught my attention: the more or less narrow margin of land written and rewritten by water. The metaphor imposed itself almost immediately. All littoral compositions known to geologists were experimented with here. The lake's power of forgetting surpassed its memory. Seeking no analogies, I wrote with my back to the lake. When the warm weather set in, however, I ran out of words.

Song Without Words

The poem rehearses its lines even as I wake
Robert Duncan

You always store pebbles under your tongue. There is no difference between root and cheek. Sublime collector without an archive, please forget the taste of milkweed and my face in the morning.

In the dream, we dance off tempo. The chorus of gulls spits abject syllables and we pick up pearls.

You have anaesthetized numbers and defied heavenly calculus. Divine excrements forge new generations. Arctic lamp nourished by gale, don't judge the bone by the weight of flesh.

We spin sand into thunder. Birds of prey alight on its branches.

You teach contempt to those who have ears and cruel caress to those who have skin. Before you, blind alleys grope for the threshold. Alpha and Charybdis, release the words trapped in mass graves.

The dream takes place entirely under water. I stitch the shores with your best yarn like a doublet.

Your hands turn letters into islands and books into lost ships. Fresh prophets augur old wars from gutted starfish. Babel of laughter, disperse my fears over the hundred and ten stories.

We fashion new rituals with our fingers. Trammellers catch in this mesh bowfin and perch.

You skim sleep from the dream and peel the skin from the mirror. Your frown is worth the empire. Boundless well, give me back the salt of my tears.

Now the dance is played in slow motion. We thieve in the interval.

Your surge meets the fall and your whirl foretells winter. Those who lend their garments to the wind enter the secret. Garden of lights, let not their last word be a scream.

We trade places on the fish market. The scales have been calibrated for the minimum of air.

You stamped your face against the sky and carved your thoughts into the ground. Pool of misery, please forget the smell of hyssop and the shape of my belly.

Migrant Song

When I come here, I come home. I do not come from here and, as I leave, it is not from here that I go. Here, I am at large. I wed the lineage of its etymologies. I translate.

The natatory fringe. My native tongue. My tactile noun. My ligament: język like jezioro, the lake I speak.

I smack my lips and lick off the pronoun. Now, not own. Rather, unlatched. Entirely here.

Swallowed. Fluent lung. Listen. Slow down. Exhale the land. I belong to the unbound. Always less. Liquidated. As Algonquin or Illinois. Quicksand sails. I come second.

Paint me a name. Unlock the articulations of the tribe. Mishigami migrant. Large gift. Long for the flood. Big water spells.

Here come the hands. Utterly speechless. New blood obliterates blood spilled. Polished graves.

Clad in stripes, star-eyed slaves. Crave the soil where to plant muscles and cod. Look, child, the water is raked with larch twigs.

Proclaim this surface a clean slate. Each crumb sinks to the mudflat. Calm water breaks the bank.

I deposit my notes in the sand. The wind pots dry leaves. Do we differ in our desires?

I come home each time I come here. I conform my path to your thirst and my thighs shape your current. Glacial ancestors.

Jorge Sanchez

Bio: Jorge Sanchez lives in Chicago with his wife and son, and teaches at Hebrew Theological College. His work has previously appeared in *Iowa Review, Indiana Review, Hotel Amerika*, and other journals. His first book manuscript, *Non-Cartoon World*, has been a finalist for the Tupelo and Dorset Prizes, and a semi-finalist for the *Crab Orchard Review* First Book Prize.

Poetic Statement:

I remember Dean Young saying once, "Content causes tension, and tension causes form." Or at least, that's what I remember him saying. That's one of those seminal insights about poetry I keep revisiting. My poetic interests are far-flung: the lyric, poetry exploring my "Cubanicity," formal experiments and traditionalist ventures that attempt to negotiate meter and rhyme in 21st Century urban America, political poetry, poetry of fatherhood, poetry of faith.

I'm not sure that any poetic statement I might write can be definitive; although I don't eschew or avoid any particular poetic program, I don't think I adhere to one either. Rhyme and meter in one poem, free verse in another, a postmodern nonce sonnet in the next. I figure if I'm bored with what I write, other readers probably will be, too. I try to keep myself on my toes.

Galway Kinnell draws a distinction between the merely personal and the truly personal, that which is of interest to one person and that which is a private experience with universal significance. If it's one thing I'm trying to walk toward, poetically, it's the latter. If there's one thing I think I'm trying to drum out of my work, it's the former.

Poem

Pope makes man the measure of things
though now the measure of a man
is the length of his shadow, the volume
of his voice, the number of people
who remember him after his visa expires.
Nowadays, people talk more about
the measure of a modem in Mbs, mega
bytes per second, each byte made of eight
bits. Before the days of computers,
computers were the dreary drudge-skulls
compiling books of logarithms. Before
the days of computers, everyone knew
eight bits meant a dollar, American
colonists cutting up Spanish doubloons,
known as pieces of eight. Wedge-shaped
money tends to make people nervous,
though. The practice did not last long.
Thus the modern dissatisfaction with cities.
The rectangles soar upwards awkwardly,
legions of condos lining the lakeshore.
Geometric things slip away easily. We remember
the puff-ball clouds but not the star fruit.
We easily recall the smallest quivering
roadside iridescence, but stumble to call
to mind a theorem, making it hard
to remember an address, a birthday,
or the name of a man you once knew well.

Baptism of Firewater, Fire and Water

Almost every night of the week we went out,
burnt to be reburnt, unredone, we went out,
trying flame against all the night, we went out,
went out and went out.

Mornings waking up in the afternoon, gone
still and bloodshot-looking, the guns put down and
light an enemy, on the day of measure,
measuring all off

This the other side of equation, side-by-
side, bananas stretched and athwart the ruler's
teeth, the ruler's stripes, and all things are unsensed,
roots in the air and

cut off: funny jackal's ungrinning maw-gape
squish and squash grape, on the tightrope and tired, so
tired, the pumpkin broken, my head in patch of
some someone's front yard,

blackeyed susans make me a crown, the legends
made of these disgraceful sonatas, songs of
songs of songs, tripped up and well done, our gooses
cooked in the gaslights.

Dawn's minute gaslights: Lake, you have fallen on me,
gone away, and bumble oh bumble bees shine,
shirts aglow, the pier now too far to reach, day
creeping near our sleeves.

Joel Craig

Bio: Joel Craig lives in Chicago, Illinois, working as a graphic designer and deejay. His poems have been published in *The Iowa Review, Fence, Spoon River, MoonLit,* and are forthcoming in the *Zoland Poetry Annual.* He co-founded and curates The Danny's Reading Series.

Poetic Statement:

When I was growing up, I was always jealous of my friends who had relationships with their grandparents. My father's parents passed away before I was born, as did my mother's father. My grandmother I met only a handful of times, so the idea of "going to grandma's house" was pure fiction to me. What could it be like to have these other homes? I think even at a young age, tripping over newly complex emotions, I constructed my fantasies out of sensory details, often minute. If I were to imagine something as trite as scoring the winning run, getting the girl, the adulation of my peers, I could never complete the image.

I'd get stuck trying to figure out what shoes were perfect for the scene, or what setting it should be played out in. What I love about writing poems is that I can engage these aspects of my imagination so equivocally. The shoes make a good metaphor for seeking the right words for a poem, but sometimes I just want the actual shoes! I used to imagine playing hide-and-go-seek at grandma's house, bumping into unexpected things, discovering secrets. Making a poem, going deeply into its new environment, gives me this thrill...even of being caught.

Street Dad

Let me try to lay out what I think I understand
        about my life. I took a sip
        of wine and plunged.

The new plague has worked so quickly we've returned
        nearly to equilibrium.

What's behind me has been built out of nothing
        into a whole row of apartments
        full of exotic people.

You can presume relative safety. I'm a quiet person.
        I don't make a lot of noise
        in public.

The most I can ever do is establish what appears to be
        a relatively safe level
        for myself, for my own body and mind.

A flash of amusement, realizing the invitation
        to pounce could be taken
        more than one way.

I have two cats who live outside hunting gophers and mice.
        There's a bit more to climb
        before we level out.

She was thin, shy and tended to be exacting and impatient,
        but I was a good, caring father.

He had the heart and clearness of mind
        to be a therapist. We could afford
        little in the way of school.

Emptying his pockets we came across
        a policy for trying out
        new groups of people.

A safe level for particular bodies, nervous systems
            and private individuals with questions.

They may be a bit uncomfortable about what
            they think I'm doing
            but they've no reason to stop me.

I used to have a dog called Bruno
            but when he died I didn't
            have the heart to replace him.

I learned what it was to be really poor, what it does
            to the human spirit.

Fundamental things still apply—
            a greenness that makes Ireland
            look grey encircling a perfect crescent bay.

A place in which only self-deluded, naïve people hope
            for things to get better. Las Vegas
            and the end of western history.

Above all is the ghost of sunk capital. Terrible assets
            that won't be born. Telling a cop
            to fuck off.

It's a strange feeling to look up the hill, across the grass and see
            those buildings staring down
            where there used to be nothing but sky and trees.

She never really said anything I could count on, and I didn't want
            to waste any more time or energy than I had to
            on people who play games.

So to you, yes. Yes for telling the truth. To your intuitive fingers
            and all the rest of you, what are you
            trying to say?

She'll be coming to be with me for a while. I'm meeting her plane
            tomorrow morning.

She's wonderfully gentle. Down the stairs into the living room, the
        fire
        is still throwing off occasional sparks.

Lit fingertips move thoughtfully
        up over the top of my shoulder
        and pause behind my ear.

Do cities decay differently in the New World?
        There's a faint touch of tease here—biological
        warfare sort of stuff. Recreation crisis.

Keep silent in deference to the possibly
        imminent end of the human race.
        Seem comfortably at ease with private images.

Of course there are different ways to terrorize
        from the sky. If he's the kind
        that gets easily irritated, I'll likely find out.

Evolution rapidly manufactures new species or subspecies
        out of their domesticates.

I didn't know I was suffering from an illness
        known as depression. For the first time
        in my life, I thought I was seeing the world.

I sat for a moment, staring at my knees as I tried
        to put broad, wide images
        into small, tidy words.

Daniel Borzutzky

Bio: Daniel Borzutzky is the author of two books, *Arbitrary Tales* (Triple Press, 2005), and *The Ecstasy of Capitulation* (BlazeVox Books, 2007). His work has been published in *American Letters and Commentary, Antennae, BlazeVox, Chicago Review, Coconut, Denver Quarterly, Fence, Golden Handcuffs Review, Kulture Vulture, La Petite Zine, LIT, LVNG, Magazine Cypress, Near South, Octopus, Pom², Shampoo, Spoon River Poetry Review, Third Bed, Word for/Word*, and several other journals.

Daniel's translation work has focused on writers from Chile. His translation of Chilean poet Jaime Luis Huenún's *Port Trakl* will be published by Action Books in 2007, and these poems have appeared in *Circumference, Fascicle, Mandorla, Action, Yes*; one poem from *Port Trakl* was selected by the Poetry Society of America for its Poetry in Motion program. It was hung on public buses in Los Angeles.

Daniel is also completing a collection of stories by a Chilean writer from the 1930s named Juan Emar, sections of which have appeared in *Conjunctions, Fence, Denver Quarterly (forthcoming), and Action, Yes*. Daniel is also working with texts by the Chilean poet Manuel Silva Acevedo, some of which have been published in *Circumference* and *Action, Yes*. Daniel teaches in the English Department at Wright College in Chicago.

Poetic Statement:

Much of my poetic work evolves through my interactions with other forms of writing. Some times these source writings are "literary," while other times the source writings come from essays, political speeches, or women's magazines and strange journalistic pieces of early 20th century Americana. In the case of "Away," I wrote it soon after seeing Caryl Churchill's great play "Far Away."

189

Away

Dear sir, wasps are circling our heads. Birds watch
our worst moments and their tweets are progress
reports to the wind. Waves are evil yet
they treat some nations more kindly. The news
says the news has disappeared. Still, we are
unsure if fog is our enemy. Wind
is against us. Rumors say fog will join
us. We watch our bodies dissolve into
fog and soon our heads are floating. Our
shadows know where our feet go, our minds do
not. Dear sir, owls are against us. We
shoot trees but the bullets pierce us. Mud is
against us. Streams are with us. Crickets and
cocoons are against us. Echoes cannot
be tamed. They hide in ditches, or in
perfect visibility, sleep is not
our friend.

Joel Felix

Bio: Joel Felix lives in Chicago where he edits the journal *LVNG* with Peter and Michael O'Leary. He is the author of the chapbooks *Catch and Release*, published by the Chicago Poetry Project, and *Monaural*, published by Answer Tag Home Press. Recent poems can be found in the Chicago Review. Joel works as an adult learning curriculum developer and is a part-time faculty member of the School of the Art Institute of Chicago.

Poetic Statement:

I am exploring the literal and metaphoric senses contained by the word environment, which I see including the orders of natural and human design. The environs circles all transactions, symbolic or otherwise; it is the very means from which experience is derived. If the poem may be said to model experience, we must also acknowledge that we *learn* via mimesis, through the reproduction of experience in art. This recognition promotes hope for an art as self-reflexive as consciousness itself. I write from the hope that the imaginal-mimetic act may keep pace with the changes in experience constant and profound.

100% Entitlement

Make sure the last words out of your name
        consist of three parts:
golf balls with basic speech
        telling, telling, and telling
again that you,
        participant, may no longer
waive the rights we imagine
        save you.
Go with seniors afraid of tripping
        on forgotten, uneven sidewalks,
search for a place to scratch off
        the word *charitable*
to find what lies beneath
        the most important two dollar charge
for this affinity.

excerpts from Service

Design 3-05

Cleaning out Mother's desk
The tape should not be screaming.

There are people
working and people we trust enough
to let.
The space inside
you rent

The back

you sleep on.

Design 6-05

Sleek, efficient partners
Come to bed.

I carried you here in my mouth.

Four large toes end each branch
in the nest on the wall.

Mother's desk is empty
but I would like to leave

one cherub behind.

Raymond Bianchi

Bio: Raymond L Bianchi, a native of suburban Chicago, is a poet and translator. His work has *appeared in Aufgabe, ACM, Birddog, 26, The Economist, Near South, Moria, Tin Lustre Mobile,* and many other journals. His first book *Circular Descent* was published by Blaze Vox Press in 2004, and his chap book *American Master* was published by Moria Books in 2005. A collection of his translations he edited and a poetry section of Brazilian poetry will appear in the spring 2007 issue of *Aufgabe* magazine.

Poetic Statement:

Poetry is something I came to in my late 20's . Unlike many poets today, I was not trained in it in school; it arose out of my life. I first learned poetry from the language around me as a child and young adult. I first heard what poetry can do as small child listening to St Francis, Dante, and Manzoni being quoted by my grandmother and other relatives.

To be a poet was something to be aspired to in my family. I first started writing when I was a volunteer in Cochabamba, Bolivia. I worked in a men's prison, and poetry came from that place. I later fell in love with poetry from all of Latin America especially the Andes and Brazil. Poetry in Latin America means something and is never solely personal which is central to my poetic ideal.

What is important to me is to read deeply and to consume as much poetry as possible. I use this reservoir of poetry to build my own poetic ideal and to always be learning more and trying to live harder. I have come to love interacting with poets to build something new.

Poetry in spite of what has happened in recent years is not a profession; one can be trained to be a poet, but there is no degree that confers on you the title Poet. All those people who have gotten MFA's thinking this piece of paper makes you a poet are mistaken. The thing that makes poetry great is intensity of living and intensity of reading. All the connections and poetic politics in the world will never replace a life well lived and many books consumed. This is what I desire to create in my poetic life.

"Leave the Gun. Take the Cannoli."

The pungency of those men who use bear
grease to keep their hair down while discussing
the Bel Canto. On that Saturday afternoon,
breasts were heaving and Comiskey Park green
was in my nose and cigarettes burned the vinyl
chairs. Hordes of monsters, offering plates of
food to garden statues next to faux
ponds. . . While talking and listening to Offenbach,
I think "fuck art, let's dance." I make a full
lunch of an Italian Beef Sandwich with nice
sport peppers and a really wet bun and date
stamping. G-string bikinis and a great piece of
steak, rare and bloody, give me indigestion and
a need for tea. The stripper's smell is in my
nose and the roof is leaking yellow National
Geographics.

"La Gioia è Mimetica"
For Antonio Porta

The frozen nosehairs fall out
And hit the pavement at 200 miles an hour
"la scatola si apre e chiude il dito"
joints are often pulled apart and the tendons are
ripped and stretched to the ends of their usefulness
San'Antonio's statue is in a church in Qing Dao, China

The Russians are the deepest poets
With texture and depth
And beet soup
God listens to prayers
But does not hear them

The Po River flows from the Alps to the Adriatic Sea
Which is where Venice is located

The listening devices that are available today are so small that they
can live
Inside you cells and know exactly what you are doing
And whom you are interacting with

Alexander Glos is a Czech married to a Russian living in Orlando
Disneyworld is reality
Calcutta is fantasy
New York is real
Charlie-horse

American Master

Counting

      noble worker

having served you

      brought you from poor wretch to rich suburbanite

The false counsel of the ungrateful

      immodest

      I renounce all I've learned here

and spit on the wood tearing my flesh

Arnold of Brescia preached against the Church taking up arms and
fighting wars.

2

Returning to Chicago after a long time away things become
apparent about the city of my formation that were not evident
before. The first thing your notice is the fact that real Chicagoans
always find a way to find out who you are-with this I mean where
you came from. There are a whole set of preconceptions that
remain strongly held in Chicago about people and where their last
name originated.

Suddenly

 become strong

        full of conviction
affix blame

proclaim a fast

solution

definite questions, movement of purpose

certain order

Compose our movement on the question; war guilt clarified in the
light of historical truth. The preliminary condition led to future
success. our movement should bring knowledge of the meaning of
peace to the minds of the popular culture.

democratic success.

dig into the mushy mud of the people
the naked truth
despicable swindle
hideousness

drip the paint outside the lines
blend the edges
remove the sharpness
crush right angles

use the brushes like sticks
paint over the door so it won't open
struggling stages
        a temptation to conform
the tactics of battle-cries
crazy conclusions
particularly strong stenches
motives found entirely illusory,
point towards the same ends

a young movement

Human fecundity a semblance of justification

Martin Luther arguing with the Pope
Francis Xavier arguing with Krishna
Hernan Cortes smashing jade idols

Chicago unlike New York is a city where the basic and the hard
won is prized and quick millions are envied but never respected.
Donald Trump must be building that big building on the river
because no one here thinks that his gold lame life is worth thinking
about.

from *Celebrated Genome*

Sliced sky
Roxanne/Persephone
hand smashed

under an anvil
small bones pressed into the anvil
Staircase ascending

cleaning guns
With bent penises
Dirty Texans

mushroom headed Listening
Grotto of Cattulus
Buon Mangiare

"The corner of 35th and Shields the Hamburg Athletic club took their
baseball bats and smashed in the skulls of the ones from across the street,
across Long John Wentworth."

Imagine Anna Akmatova
With a bucket of shit
Sloshing down the stairs-no verse for her

A poet's prerogative
a clean
Cesspool in which to write

Nelson Algren
William Allegrezza both devotees
Of Gary with steel shards

Sean Connery said it is necessary to hit women
It gives them sense
He is a Man

rough and place a cigarette

Out in the ashtray
Give me some good Hemingway hardness

Henry Miller
Slap him Hard!
And scream without irony

"Fuck em"

Luft Post
field composting
'1969' cement

broken out of the earth
smooth round
river stones

Broken roots
Rotten wood
Smells like tea

Torn Open leaves
Light Small sounds
Of bells-campagnille

the air of
Monastic listenings
Chinese food boxes

opened intestines
Memorial Day for
Small slices

Cynthia Bond

Bio: Cynthia Bond was not born, but was mostly raised, in downstate Illinois. After receiving a Bachelor's degree in English and Rhetoric from the University of Illinois, Urbana-Champaign, Bond traveled extensively in India and Europe. Bond has an MFA in poetry from Cornell University where she taught writing and directed a literary research and publication project for Henry Louis Gates, Jr. Bond received a JD from Cornell Law School, where she has also taught. Bond writes poetry, fiction, film criticism and literary criticism. Her publications include a bibliography of 19th Century African-American women writers for Oxford University Press. In addition to appearing in magazines, Bond's poetry is in *The Best American Poetry 1994*. Bond's latest publication on law and film appears in *The Cumberland Law Review*. Bond lives in Chicago where she works as a law professor.

Poetic Statement:

"Documentary" is from a cycle of short lyrics which were composed one a day for about a year. The inspiration for these poems was that each day would end with the writing of a poem. This project allowed me to imagine I was limited by the day's events, thus making my day about a poem, and poems ostensibly about my days. In this and every project, there is no freedom beyond form.

Documentary

In one super saturated reality, the
angle cuts from a gun metal length
of op-art thigh to phone larger than
crisp crossed ankles next. Nature,
on one coast and the other, has taken
different rancors on. The earth's
digestion tossed you from your
somnambulant soap in the shower; memories
of crushing underpasses rifled the
downtown area, so execs checked in from
hidden holiday homes. Calm, ever
calmer here I told you: except for lunchtime
conjuring of fabricated magentas and
lapis, the clouds played out, in multious
theaters, picture postures various.
Over east, the bluest lift of liquid
in starchy bowls of clouds.
To west, the books of resurrection
in the sun drawing water through. And north,
and south.

William Allegrezza

 **Bio:** A native of Mississippi, William Allegrezza came to Chicago after finishing work on his Ph.D. in Comparative Literature. His articles, reviews, translations, and poems have been published in numerous countries, and he has published many books, chapbooks, and e-books of poetry, including *Ladders in July, In the Weaver's Valley, Covering Over, Temporal Nomads, The Vicious Bunny Translations, Ishmael Among the Bushes*, and *Lingo*. He edits the e-zine *Moria* (www.moriapoetry.com) and is the co-founder of Cracked Slab Books.

Poetics Statement:
A poem pushes us just outside what we know using language at once familiar and made strange. What we hear matters. What we read matters. What we imagine matters. As a poet, all those things filter into the poem as I sit with chaos and pull fragments from the semi-conscious realm of creativity. At times the sound, syllable, word, and line cohere; beyond that point, I have little control.

seeking hades again

in some dream i find myself watching

cars   people
               villages   trees   life
      aid   juries
     love

and somewhere below
a bell cord is being pulled and shadows
                          are gathering
                            before a pit
                            where i should
                            seek answers.

quarter

"quarter tuttle leads environmental placation"

la plaz or new orleans
                  "utter banality. oh. oh. oh"
"asses, this city is being lead by asses."
                    12. . .9. . .34 . . .67

"really not worth the hassle. I mean at 7:15 she calls for the paper.
what does she think I am?"

one man works his way forward on the stage while a woman in
bright orange makes clicking noises. another man sits cross-legged
on a slightly raised platform (about three feet high). in the
background, a drum beats the rhythm to taps.

       "have you ever seen something so crazy? be just like a live
       talk show traveling in there"

"yo quiero"

"do you have the time?"
                    ab . . . d . . .qr

"rye stations leave red on the news"

"could have been you falling from the rail"

* answer the questions.
* fold and staple the form 4281 to form 8756.
* make sure to sign the bottom of each.
* do not include cash.

a question

why are you always here
reading over my shoulder
disbelieving that i can
see shadow turn into
shadow and flowers in
fields that i have never
seen or swifts over
vineyards that might
never have existed or have been
gone for thousands of years
or that in geârdagum makes as
much sense as anything
i could say just now
as if words themselves
can explain why the
silence continues to echo
in rooms that i create
with time and language
rooms that i cannot
inhabit except through
doing as you are doing
just now?

replacements

i am sick   with patient
women gathered round to listen

birds flying fall dead   earth   shakes

my dreams foretell   full storm
coming   ships wandering lost
days on end   with fear and bewilderment

in excelsis   someone sings to someone else

to found a colony one must
begin in blood
        i am covered with it.

grackle or grace

grackle   or grace the straight line grows curved through the screen
and the irregularities of light and shadow become pine and cedar
no reason for confusion four plus four minus eight is zero   simple
to conceptualize relation trust the old riddle   it takes two to make a
poodle

re latin g   th e   sir ens scre am p ul ling the han ds in to
th e burnin g co re of a ci ty rid dle d by destru ction in to
ey es th row n fr om cradd ling head s or visio n or buildings
over turned pul ling into re pla cin g int o   ball   concrete
                                    handles   numbers
                                    chaos   wood
                                    lines   tears

the tree once cut and laid becomes a window with eyes either side
so easy to see or is it settled upon like dusty couches in beach
houses though we would expect it to sing through muddy layers
with light the bronze mask at the bottom of the river is silent in
corrosion.

Jennifer Karmin

Photo credit: Amina Cain

Bio: Jennifer Karmin is a poet, artist, and educator who has published, performed, exhibited, taught, and experimented with language throughout the U.S. and Japan. She is a founding member of the public art group Anti Gravity Surprise, curator with the SpareRoom time-arts cooperative, and co-host of the Red Rover reading series. Jennifer teaches creative writing to immigrants at Truman College and works as a Poet-in-Residence for the Chicago Public Schools. She recently started teaching poetry to incarcerated youth. Studying with Robert Creeley, Susan Howe, Charles Bernstein and many other generous creative minds, she earned degrees from SUNY Buffalo and the School of the Art Institute of Chicago. For over seven years, she has been a proud resident of Chicago's Humboldt Park neighborhood.

Poetic Statement:

My poetry stems from curiosity, a search exploring the endless possibilites of language. Intersecting writing with sound and image, I produce new forms for the page. I uncover communication: pushing, pulling, taking language apart, putting it back together again and finding places for all of the missing pieces. Inspired by collage techniques, I traverse multiple sources. At present, I am developing a series of poems about the lives of Joan of Arc, Harriet Tubman, and Helen Keller. I have been researching each of the women's lives, contemplating the ways illness transforms history, and examining the elements as catalysts for change: fire, air, water and earth. To survive is to communicate - belong, belonging, keep going.

cultural imagination

image visual language is not always linear how to interact with a place non place learning to see to look have nothing interact commodity exchange wanting to see to shoot the camera after being captured by native americans some white people did not want to go back had to be taken back in chains wrote ben franklin there is something disconcerning the globalization of michael jordan collective memory giving to a place to get back pre existing narrative structure linear space it's not the joke but how you tell it experience is a creative act knowledge is appropriation active looking to participate in your spaces no direct experience except self the future is a good thing to have memory is sharing stories permission tourists only meaning continues to evolve visual notes a physical action absence of conjunctions don't forget what is strange metaphor anticipates performance that's nonsense that's everyday life

water / helen

satisfying
thirst   water balance
needs
desires
                                                water guide

(i lived
myself
into all things)   water language

our flood
leak   water organ
flowing in

a channel   water room
a conduit

colorless
tasteless
odorless
transparent

water spirit

earth / now

ground composed of
planet inhabited by

earth crossing

burial
capture
plunge
conceal

earth history

earth hunger

(please do not
do that
to me)

earth noise

shape
where we
dwell

earth time

present
abode

earth tongue

Tim Yu

Bio: Tim Yu was born in Evanston, grew up on the North Side and the North Shore, and now lives in Hyde Park. His collection *Journey to the West*, which won the Vincent Chin Memorial Chapbook Award from Kundiman, was published as part of the Winter 2006 issue of *Barrow Street*. His poems and essays have appeared in *Chicago Review, Meanjin, SHAMPOO,* and *2nd Avenue Poetry*. He can also be found in Toronto, where he is an assistant professor of English at the University of Toronto, or online at http://tympan.blogspot.com.

Poetics statement:

Each city has its own distinctive language; the question is where to find it. I've tried to look at those words that get most taken for granted: place names, streets, and stations, words that seem purely instrumental and yet are rich enough to form, in their various arrangements, a map of the landscape, or a hidden history. In "Elephant & Castle," the stations of London's Underground offer an urban genealogy that's both pastoral and violent, while "Loop" is animated by the more urgent rhythms of Chicago's Ciceros, Cermaks, and Pulaskis. Working with these limited palettes allows new constellations to emerge, making poetry a guide to both the city we know and the one we might imagine.

Elephant & Castle [12]

Dart on
king's land, put

knee bridge over
shepherd's bush. Prevail

when the rich man
crosses, chewing

tough nails and
perusing stone.

Ham's broad
of back, stepped

like green
mom. Clap

hands, shelve
arses back.

I'm Pretty Sure Bison Art

rules the rails, pretty

tracings holding
in the darkened station.

No smoking gun
from the shitpile, nor

hard-bore lender dubbed
man-in-charge. Zoom

up over babbling

park, where even

tour-bus traffic
lulls. Your sneakered

feet go ringless,
running in place.

It is this red-moon
doggerel that rises,

wary, over
the tuning eye.

Laura Sims

Bio: Laura Sims's first book of poetry, *Practice, Restraint,* was the recipient of the 2005 Fence Books Alberta Prize. She is also the author of four chapbooks, including *Bank Book* (Answer Tag Press, 2004) and *Corrections* (Bronze Skull Press, 2006). She has received two Pushcart Prize nominations for her poems, and was awarded First Prize in the 2004 Summer Literary Seminars Writing Contest, which provided a one-month residency in St. Petersburg, Russia. She was recently awarded a Japan-US Friendship Commission / NEA Creative Artist Exchange Fellowship to spend six months in Japan in 2006. Individual poems have appeared in the journals *First Intensity, 26, How2, 6X6, Columbia Poetry Review, jubilat, LIT, Boston Review,* and *3rd Bed,* among others. She lives in Madison, Wisconsin, where she teaches creative writing and composition.

Poetic Statement:

A productively spacious poem speaks in the space(s) as potently as it speaks in the words themselves.

Space on the page = space in the day & in the world.

I wrote most of the "Bank" poems in the dead space of an office between menial tasks.

The poems are about: work, money, water, loss, cars, isolation, love, nature v. man, insanity, death, survivor's guilt, war, time, desperation, bodies, beauty, sickness, ironic occurrences, torture, disappointment, housework, joy, murder, motherhood, branding, imperialism, inexplicable violence, Spaniards, sex, old age, disappearance, abandonment, mysticism, tidal waves, longing, spiritual connection, institutionalization, and MRIs.

They co-opt other people's stories and world events to a large extent, but the space is mine.

BANK SEVEN

Tit for tat

Your border *gives in*

      Under the wet awning, a bomb

Or something

We think—

      We were animals

Friend

BANK THIRTY-THREE

There were balustrades

There

And water filming the smooth interior wall

Time for coloring in

(A gown, a car)

There you sit in a room

Subdued

Roberto Harrison

Bio: Roberto Harrison's most recent books include *Counter Daemons* (Litmus Press), *Os* (subpress), and *Elemental Song* (Answer Tag Home Press), all published in 2006. He was born in Corvallis, Oregon, in 1962, to Panamanian parents. A few months after his birth, he and his family moved back to Panama, where they lived until he was seven. In 1969, he and his family moved to Delaware. His first language was Spanish, and he did not begin learning English until arriving in Delaware. He has lived in various places throughout the United States, including Boston; Bloomington, Indiana; and San Francisco. He now lives in Milwaukee, Wisconsin, where he works as a systems librarian. He edits *Crayon*, with Andrew Levy, and the Bronze Skull Press chapbook series.

Poetic Statement: Cocuyito (Firefly)

      I write to unravel emotional knots that belong to no one, to grow into space, and to see, as a viewer of I.T., and as a person of people, what might be learned of animals, pebbles, insects, ferns, and digitalia. As the nervous system of a cockroach is decentralized, (one can smash its head and it will walk away), what is seen is seen, now more clearly, in a vast network with fewer and fewer holes, lights are on and off. Two languages make two twins: the virtual and the real, North America and South America (with Central America as a bridge), the on and the off, the sun and the moon, the poles of the earth and of the inside. The world is short, the world arriving is long. This is the story, a circle, and the cradle, of an atom. Signs are not the only thing a human mouth is made for, signs are what the eyes put into balance, signs are the flood that root the calm in every season. Winter makes the silence for the loudness of the summer, fall makes graveyards for the spring to grow in.

ritual number

the 3 of rooms
for a space
in the caravan
that a thinning
horse
sleeps through

the 3 of faces
that a river bleeds
for fish, alone

the 3 for 4
in words
that stretch
a gown
equating, it's a motor
from the smiling
vision
that extends
the firing squad
for seeing

the 3 for 4
in one
without a semblance
that a rowing makes,
a 2
under the wave

a 4 for seven
that beside yourself
makes many
for the hearse
to come
for children, flat
on locked down plains
they fire out
feet

of repetition

a seven for an empty
view, or the sea
that never reels
the beds, on the clotted
pulse
that a mother
bombs

an eight that every
eye
interrogates,
the continent
for countless clouds
in the aftermath
of earthquakes

the one unknown
for 9, the hands
for planting each
in ruins
that a flower
spreads
to see
the night

the 10 because
a 7 knows, in
each removal
that a winter
solves to wear,
under a tree
that many sell
for younger suns

eleven on
a click,
in the petals
of a face

appearing
in the hallways
of a shattered
reliquary, done
for others gone
to heal
the technicality
that nothing is

a 12 for every
mote that carves
an action
on the trail
that most removes
the palms
from pockets
in the fear
that fire
resembles

13
for memories
that make
a new one
of coyotes
filled with shirts
in fruits
that peel
Before

2 sevens
for the hands
that make a flesh
arrive without
a word
in snows
and settlements
that many know
to ring
a perfect

Zero

●

the 2 an end
for foam
that evenings
plug
to play
the woman
in a letter
that acidic
words
can be

the 2 a faltering
that honey
fits
to tire the green
that wheels
return,
a window
that the trust
will make
to burn
the moth
again

the 2 a tree lined
fruit
that slaughter makes
erasing
what a miniscule
embrace
will see
betrayed
to give
the sound
— a touch

mandan (they send)

like the lost car that a river knows
like the heat of an ointment in pinpoints of breathing
like the unknown western in mountains of tar
like a knot in each word for comfort
like a horse on a face with four hooves
like the knives that a heart squirms into
like the feel that the last day pushes, that a fire paints red
like the shower that a plain divides in snakes
like a frozen torso pining for food
like the ammunition that a pair of wings makes dry
like a shirt that plants seeds under worn out skin
like the clouds of mistakes, pouring through sleep
like the walls that crack open
like a wake in a spin
like the exits of oceans that a salmon knows
like the dust that is written with number
like a trust full of beacons of light
like the negative shade of a fungus
like the promise that a lie gives out
like the pulse of a trap
like the rainbow that cuts off a hand
like a psychic intent full of negative calls
like salt for the season that covers the fields with jail
like the round word that a star pisser pulls

like the plains that a crossed out calendar day will mourn
like the fate of the wrong side of talking
like hills under snow that a letter revolves
like the husky reflections of leeches that writhe
like a sword in Toledo
like the animals growing a vent in a cage
like the sequence of nights dropping straw for a cipher
like the trade in the fair full of cycles and ends
like the cattle that heat all the drains with green grass
like the nipples of outdoor intentions
like a wing on the door that a glass makes arise
like the underground fluid of digitized words
like the ice in a cavern

like a ride through the green light of dying
like the yellowish herd of relational cards
like the face that a wallet becomes
like the wrong line of radios making a rule
like the crust on the last day of hunger
like the rodeo riding the real for a cut
like the cells in the spread of the fall
like an ape for the circle of color
like reflections that turn on a wheel
like the freezer of sweethearts
like a change for the current that makes a return
like the pause on the shore full of rattles
like the oxygen tent making holes in a lung

the face
of friendly fire
is knotted
for a smile
deleted
for a smile
that saves
the executioner

the face
intended
jail, by rocking
through the holes
that fear
the clear blue
family
of dots

the face
resembles
next to nothing
in the network
full of incremental
touches
that a string
intends to limit

by the light

the face
of arctic
evolutions, a hunt
that people came
to read
instead of mapping
all the flights
of sleep
without a sound

the face
of terrible returns
will fade
outside the pouring
crowd
of animal
relation
in the mineral
of wealth

the face
of providence
is making shores
for surfers
in the foam
of magnifying
eyes
that are the opposite
of winter calm

the face
is never there
in each intention
that the worst
reliance
knows to ask
for heat

the face
is after
every opening
that makes
a number
count
for all
of what is good

like a robot that falls and makes good for a switch

like the breasts of a mop that soaks blood

like a magnifying glass for the sun

like the picture of radar in space

like a misery flood on the phone

like electrical laughter that the pointed shake

like enemies held in a double embrace

like extinctions returning

like a handshake of style for the heat

like the flower that bottles a fly for a mouth

like the still dunes of dust on a beautiful girl

like the crack in an oven

like a moon that gets brighter with age

tandem

the wake before the open half of creaking sounds
makes many of the drops that color each horizon,
planted in a trap with springs, a newer
shower in the veins that travel in a sharpened
match that's made for mornings that will run. a poison

valley that a schoolboy carves into a number, floods
equations that the moisture in a word will float
beside each quarry, in the diver that a prehistoric
predator remains inside, to weaken in the tar. a wall
that fleas remind the crystallizing harpist on a wave

believes and walks beside a conversation that the steel
for stiff instruction wades without the newly born,
the boat that means its triangle is crowded, for a hand
in measurements that flock to rain the cattle's wood
to seals and networked crones inside a better visit

for a rule. a miser and a mystery can run outside
each frothing cold without its only shower in the snow, its one
together with a mine, within magnetic moons that cross
the promises in each of its intentional receivers, windy
camps filled full with intersections and a view. choose

the mountain hollowed out into volcanoes, highways
split, received, to warn the heat that settles on the floor
grown out from our dismembered moon, the settlement
that promises will stagger in the evening of a mark
in showers that a particle in each of the deliveries of one

of the installments of another life can make to stand
in open sightings for the keyed in explanation, for the way
that lips improve upon a square. the razing house that makes
another cave into a safe, a winter cut into for roots
of knotted up relations that a people plant to make a friend

of rupture, in the backward crescent fusing the intention
for a link, a pan, a service on its rainy mornings spent

226

beside the incantation of a war, a plastic wrap revealed
to wear the down in flying insects, like the quiet flight
of owls. remember that the weekend full of murders

can equate itself with noonday visits by a desert
growing through the magnified intention of a breath,
deceived and planted with a heart, a parallel envisioning
a corky shame will aim to see. shoveled out
of youngish visits in a face reflected on, a tied in two

reconnaissance that infinite relations crowd inside
for petty streets to shine away with rain, absorb
the fattened insurrection that a song divides
to see the wound that other servants make the protocol
implant a kindness as a weapon for the naked in a pool

of two's intent, the hard and metal guides that flood
a life that's weak and aimed at making food of spineless
caravans and marches through the bowl that's full
of residential perforations. a canister that spins around
and marks the next in line to die, promises a day

will never be as full as night, as empty as the hands
that soldiers carve themselves to listen, to the fire that peels
against the signals that a river full of doubt rehearses for the answer
that a people in the snow assemble for the overhaul
a center wants to crash. a viral, still foundation that a flaw

resembles, starts with following the technical delivery of holes
and gleaming cuts that several gowns and empty stalls
resend their focuses and links for raw encounters, for the bear
that once intended negative replies for light. make the seed
a running coat that, legless, can invent a shower in a virtual

relation for the once in sequence, once the followed, its second
apparition through the body of a wordless stance. solid indiscretions,
like direction, can define identity for groups that negatives
repair, a fallen log inside extinguished friends that wilderness
remakes into for longing, for the sewer that a memory, a blue

replacement for the promise of an ended name, removes. a name
that people wash into for corners cut outside the sound
that it might be, a magnet in the heart that he becomes, nothing
settled in the carriers that sold the only time intended
for the arrogant and calm. what do people in their pedestals

and calcified regurgitations do for them that settle
for a horse, a window, newer standards that communications
fold into for energy. a run that fakes the bird that promises
a view to stop inside a car, a winnowed plain that stiffs
vocabularies in a manager, and in a heart concatenated,

salivating on the door. you, grower of a pain that folds into
itself, sewer of the laughter that a tiny ball can see
to bounce us through the light, a highway
less than water in its easy flight through desperation,
like the people that a purity in one resolve can make to ratify

a simple course, the racetrack full of fuzzy fire, can go away
and die into the particle that rattles, for the nest of slowed
down tigers that the underground intent of limbless
rulers, like the maggot under crowns, the season
that correction, like a bomb that knew that he was called

a death for others, for the sleeping cow that tumbles
through a winter in return. fail, inside a segmentation full
of baubles, in the orient that flowers through the expiration
full of rested eels. one won't ever have to reach, to be a flame
of evil, in the wads that fever places for a twice together

breathing in the dark. a network integrated for the shower
in a lifeline for the willing, pink and orange in the sky, in cracks
that break a bottle in affection, in the tracks,
a roving hunter sends to you her plans, a wooden desk
is leveled, with water in the fuel of little bombs. magnetic

clips inside the rib cage of the recently forgotten, push
out pointers for the hanging plant that never knew
the love that shrank and battled its demise, to stiffen
in the halter of a flesh filled rain, carved by a remission

of the cancer of the good. networks for the radios

that cause a democratic hash to beacon – it's alive
with welts that make a criminal a stretched out limb,
a salvaging of this, your twice together goat, make
the rain its own, its weary system full of all
the crowded intersections, all the coins that one day

flag the truth and give out steady farms for ounces
full of heat and cowardice. a strong relation to the weak
can give you countries many more than friends,
when equilateral intent refuses its primordial
report for tropics in the palms of tiny plants. the cost

of rackets cut into for visits to the family and openings
that fewer words can see through, for a bag that sells
the breathing rites to any wanderer that settles
in the plain, enforcing an amendment to agreements
that the steady flow of friendly shores can make to end

the sun in shriveled up replies, for solitude that's loud
with other games, in films that write a welcome
for their own impending knives that sit, a freezer full of magic
lambs – a dozen birds that fill the air with arrows
watching horses breathe. the steps into the night that follow

go again presenting time, and come again to rest in resignations
full of silent clouds that many walk to give the light
its nails. a crowd that pulls the star from outer reaches
in the penitent and hiding, cuts the winter from the agonizing
spring. a sheet of blue can shiver off the visit to a cliff

and promise that the circuit on the forehead of the newly gone
will place a field, the causeway, other parties in the sand
and make its unknown lips drop through the pearls
and land into beginnings full of cattails, in the visit
that will feed the wilderness its vain attention to the fern

Brenda Cárdenas

Bio: Brenda Cárdenas' chapbook of poems *From the Tongues of Brick and Stone* was published by Momotombo Press (Institute for Latino/a Studies, University of Notre Dame) in 2005, and her full-length book *Boomerang* is forthcoming from Bilingual Review Press. She also co-edited *Between the Heart and the Land: Latina Poets in the Midwest* (MARCH/Abrazo Press, 2001). Cárdenas' work has appeared in a range of publications, including *Poetic Voices Without Borders* (Gival Press), *U.S. Latino Literature Today* (Longman), *Bum Rush the Page: A Def Poetry Jam* (Three Rivers Press / Random House), *Prairie Schooner*, *RATTLE*, and the *Poetry Daily* web site, among others. Ten pages of her poetry are forthcoming in *The Wind Shifts: New Latino Poetry* to be released by the University of Arizona Press this year. With Sondio Ink(quieto), a spoken word and music ensemble, she co-produced the CD *Chicano, Illnoize: The Blue Island Sessions* in 2001. Cárdenas has collaborated on a number of interdisciplinary performance art projects, including *Oh Goya, Goya!* with dancer Evelyn Vélez Aguayo (The Institute for Contemporary Arts in London, England) and *Undesirable Elements* with Ping Chong (The Chernin Center for the Arts in Chicago). Among her honors are two Illinois Arts Council finalist awards. Cárdenas holds an M.F.A. in Creative Writing from the University of Michigan and currently teaches at Milwaukee Area Technical College.

Poetic Statement:

      Mine is a hybrid poetics—a cultural and artistic fusion or the blending of various elements with an attention to the juxtapositions among them. This has lead me to work in inter-lingual and interdisciplinary spaces, including performance art and installation, as well as writing poems for the page. A number of my poems concern both cultural and personal transformation via syncretism, mythmaking, and the multi-voiced re-visionings of particular histories.

Regardless of a poem's structure, I am most bent on discovering its musical phrasings, deep images, and the turns both are willing to risk. For example, my "laywoman's" interest in linguistics led me to write a series of four impressionistic meditations on various sounds in the Spanish language. Here, I attempt to use images to capture sounds and their physical and emotional landscapes. In these and other poems, I work in, around, and between languages. Some poems are written completely in English, others in Spanish, and many in an inter-lingual blend of the two languages. When I choose to blend English and Spanish, I do so to maximize the potential of the hybrid language that resides within me, not primarily to capture a "home" language, but rather to experiment with the harmonies, dissonances, and rhythmical nuances that emerge via the patois.

For me, poems must live as much in the body as they do in the mind and, most readily, in the visceral space between the two. Perhaps, among art forms, dance is the most obvious embodiment of this, where both the sonic and the visual are always in motion. Dancers may appear still at moments, but are never really static, for there is something we (the viewer / reader) are watching and something we (add the dancer / poet) are feeling in our very muscles, and there is always the breath of all involved. Poems are always moving, changing shape, by virtue of how the elements in them interact with one another. Therefore, I'd like to make poems that change every time one reads them, not simply because the reader has come to the poem anew, but because the poem itself invites the reader to venture down, and even to create, different twists and turns along the poem's spine. I want to tattoo poems so that they bend, rise, twist, and disappear with each movement of the canvas. And eventually, I want them to move off the canvas like improvisational dances.

If
(for Roberto)

Cobalt dusk
Icicles break   free
                    from our collar bones,
                            ribs,
                                    pelvic branches,
perfect pearls of light.

Bathe me
        in fresh water eyes. When the doubt
in the *if* that is this

                noun
                    floods your alone,

            sit in the radiator's steam and hiss,
                    allow it to give you your breath.

        Then pour it
                        out the window.

        Melt my snow,
so I don't have to shovel *if's*.   No turn
                in the woods is wrong
                        when you follow
                                the tracks of something
                        that follows you,

            links end to beginning. Infinity.
                In fin,   it swims forever.

            Half empty, half empathy,
                    if is a tender conjunction.

    You tell me to trust the unfinished clauses
                    spilling from the highest branches
                        into my lap.

232

They are not patterns; they are snowflakes.
They are not feathers; they are flight.

I tell you to trust the unfinished nest
they fall from
in the Spring that has not yet arrived.
There is nothing arbitrary about it—

that circle of twigs and litter,
rinds, hair and apple blossoms
kissed like some ancient glyph
by the sun.

Song

You shout my name
from beyond my dreams,
beyond the picture window
of this Rosarito beach house.
Rushing from bed to shore
I glimpse their backs—
volcanoes rising out of the sea.
Your back, a blue-black silhouette,
feet wet with the wash of morning waves.
Fountains spring from mammal minds,
my hands lifting a splash of sand.
I'm on my knees,
toes finding a cool prayer
beneath them, fingers pressing
sea foam to my temples,
while you open arms wide as a generation,
raise them to a compass point,
dive.
If you could reach them,
you would ride their fins
under the horizon,
then surf the crash of waves

left in their wake.
And if I could grasp
my own fear,
I'd drown it,
leave it breathless and blue
as this ocean,
as the brilliant backs
of whales
surfacing
for air

Stacy Szymaszek

Bio: Stacy Szymaszek is the author of *Emptied of All Ships* (Litmus Press, 2005) as well as several chapbooks including *Mutual Aid* (gong, 2004) and *Pasolini Poems* (Cy Press, 2005). After working at Woodland Pattern Book Center in Milwaukee, WI for many years she moved to New York to be the Program Coordinator at the Poetry Project at St. Mark's Church. She edited *Gam: A Survey of Great Lakes Writing* which lived for 4 issues, before it remanifested as *Gam*. She also works as co-editor or contributing editor on various projects including Instance Press and *Fascicle*. Her current work in process is called "hyperglossia," parts of which can be found on the Internet, as a Belladonna* chapbook and forthcoming from Hot Whiskey Press.

Poetics Statement:

My idea of poetics includes confronting regimes with my mind, body, language and love. I am embroiled in the potentialities (both realized and latent) of poetry as a form of social change. To quote Oppen, "poetry is related to / music and cadence and therefore to the / force of events." In the poem I want to transform the impact of stress into vision, creating an agora for otherness and environments of persistent appeal.

horn and space

distilled to
repetition
of a word

ghost on
French horn

from my
lexicon

the sound
means

you

three times
with a lisp

changes the shape
of the space

inside

airy assembly
of ink

your
name
on an
index
card

care
for
you

in

another
script

see it
in the
tree
year

branch
character

horn and space

no occasion
for a new
vocal

metal
wind

carves
into a desk
at a plains
school

an initial
"S"

where I
have never
read

She

She sees it
in the sky

not me

Scytale

our cadre
all have one

in addition
to the cell

"I love you"
in telephone
dial code

to compliment
the unspoken

a crank radio
with cell charger

there are no dog
friendly motels
in Brooklyn

convey this
to SB

that code
tells me
how deeply

plan for
Philadelphia
and a pound
of jerky

when she bit
my lip it was

in lieu of

cracking a
practice riddle

I can agitate
a vending machine
for thanksgiving
duffle bag

prior to
a call to mom
sorry I can't
be with you

instead I say
"yes, fish stew"

my birth
certificate is
sealed in plastic

with a dog's
proof of rabies
vaccination

direct this
to JM

when I hear
the dialing 4-5-6-8-3...
I feel I belong

wherever there is
a piece of equipment

on the L train
with its new
superhuman
conductor

Chuck Stebelton

Bio: Chuck Stebelton was born in Grand Rapids, MI on March 7, 1970 and raised in the city of Wyoming. The feathered ogre lives there. He left in 1991 and earned a B.A. in a trade at Michigan State University. He discovered small press poetry while living in Boulder, CO from 1993 to 1995, then moved to Chicago in 1995 and lived there nearly two years before he could meet the middle western day again with anything like dignity. Self-published chapbooks include *The Both of Them*, *Two Dot Merkin*, and *A Fickle Sonance / A Minor Sea*. He organized the Myopic Poetry Series from 2003 to 2006. In 2005, Tougher Disguises published his first book, *Circulation Flowers*, winner of the 2004 Jack Spicer Award, and Answer Tag Home Press published *Precious*. He lives in Milwaukee and works as Literary Program Manager at Woodland Pattern Book Center.

Poetic Statement:

My hope is that there are always friends and neighbors around who are interested. I count on them being there to heckle when a poem isn't up to the task of cultivating an eloquent silence. The span of the last few years, especially my time at Woodland Pattern, has been a real saturation job. I'm happily crushed by my reading list. But along the way it's been important to keep my hand in occasional outside pursuits. Collaborations with choreographer Selene Carter (*In Leaves* and *9 Bob Dylan Songs*) led to an ensemble role in an adaptation of Tom Spanbauer's novel *The Man Who Fell In Love With The Moon* and performances with choreographer Julie Mayer (*Repository*), and with Asimina Chremos (*Orderly*). More recently I worked with Cindy Loehr on *Revival*, 'a cathedral of flame with a pre-recorded oration inside,' and her sculpture installation *Fuel for Constant Light*, a project that treaded the fine line between close correspondence and collaboration. Play is essential in itself, but just as important is the perspective gained from engaging with creative activity outside of the work. It brings home the point that poetry is there for the interested.

The Nineties

Between 1929 and 1941

without changes, without an Ars

turned to summer and all

sold to the little peeps as pets

between 1939 and 1951

often hardens, so windows snow

collective desires to collect and share

between 1949 and 1961

twenty eight leap years ago
thirty head of lamb, sheep

between 1929 and 1941

between 1959 and 1971

Foil Blossom

A squared bee scared. Equals see squared bees.

All orange blossoms have to do is act naturally.

I burn brightly and human tongues press the night.

Countertops on the day before a holiday time fences.

I modeled it. She modeled you. Lines are the topic

on Tuesday. Weaponry is the topic on Monday.

Before the very fourth there was stability in instability.

A sliver of clarity held down the chances nasturtium

had at keeping title once clover started in homing.

Ypso Bysmal

Backward prancing Thoth off a cliff

The utopian relieved over solo & ensemble

No trees cherry blossoming alone

ritual indecency on a flip diagnosis

That in everyone's heart there is a slumbering

squirrel. There a cold, ferocious lurks

Giants your size are sexy

Garden plants like automatic writing

Music will cradle some into talking

Chronic become in time as paraquat

A quick shot of silver still

recently wooded, still convivial bay

Music Without Words

My ladies can't remember les fins des
siècles. Like foxes behind fences

Decker clocked spume du Monde.

Harps were less humble
when I was a mortal.

Music for film loops
your very own working saint

there is no slot to quarter. One
blow apostrophes another.

Forever keeps changing the length
of drought. An Aesopic

fable tells the tale of a fowler deceived
by the very loudness of cicadae.

We survivors can recall the aughts.

The pizzicato blew my quote.

And bootless make the breathless
whose landmark rubble movie

near this couple, this kill courtesy

made slow company. Twenty

years and the spring is over.

Cover me in pink famous.
No one falls asleep alone.

The dulcet organization of tones

by autumn a single tone.

Jordan Stempleman

Bio: Jordan Stempleman is the author of *Their Fields* (moria, 2005) and *What's the Matter* (Otoliths, 2007). He lives in Iowa City with his wife and daughter.

Poetic Statement:

My poetry may not be typically un-American, or at least when it doesn't count, not always true: but I do think it borrows formal constrictors which, even when not overused by un-American poets, discover some way to wrangle themselves into such groupings from Misty & anti-Fugitive, to those unknown conditions like Hired Chance, Blameless, or Gospel.

> Repeatedly building on one listening.
> Repeatedly building on the sounds of ideas,
> sounds that make objects,
> sounds met by statements, as
> to become artifactual
> enough to speak for themselves…

A Fable

and when a soft-side came about
with its own chemistry, its own system
to project a sweeter legend than
what it actually lived, there will be time
to go away, assured that all thinking
makes a place that is vulnerable
and uneasy, where understanding means
something else, an entirety moving
through the branches, a dim bear
ousted by a road that now whips
over the hills, nothing covered but the
obvious: a road, a bear, a tree, some wind,
so empty without these things

Double as Bed

I am not featuring pessimism
as a function. I am not a member of a trade
union, although I was invited to a lunch
or two I meant to attend, but didn't.
The heroic, *are* the overlapping
voices found wandering the streets,
since they all came to the neighborhood too early
and the restaurant doesn't open
until noon. The city-life is back to
evolving. I know it's a central force to my reasoning
and order. There are times to go in.
This is one of those times. I am not
imagining we'll ever be together, although we
could, and so I may now begin thinking
in this sense, since taught early enough: never waste a being-
based aesthetic. That's me—
reminding myself to work, live, and then
speak, in that order. They are closest to my biological
likeness, they too have accidents as well.

Fires

The children, too young to escape
themselves, were wheeled out of the burning preschool
by attendants in their cribs. This appeared
to those who drove by, as not a catastrophe, but
as a protest of ninety screaming children wishing for freedom
from naptime.

Afterword

When we set out to edit this anthology, we knew that it would be a difficult task. Chicago has many different literary scenes, and we did not want to exclude any type of innovative writing. We searched among the various academic haunts of poetry, the University of Chicago, the University of Illinois at Chicago, the Loop colleges like Columbia College and the Art Institute, but we also found ourselves metaphorically wandering the streets of neighborhoods like Wicker Park, Logan Square, and Pilsen looking for poets.

We do not make any claims at having crafted a comprehensive anthology of Chicago's poetry—the city is too diverse for that, but we have presented, we feel, a portal through which you might begin to see the poetry scene in a high moment, so that you might see the lights of the prairie when they are shining brightly, and they are now, for Chicago and its surrounding areas are undergoing a rebirth in experimental writing. One could argue that what is being seen is the effect of fabulous teachers like Paul Hoover and Michael Anania or is the aftermath of an influx of poets from cities like New York, St. Louis, San Francisco, or Memphis. Indeed, several critics have termed this period of growth the New Prairie Renaissance, and while we are not certain that a specific school has arisen in Chicago, we are convinced that myriad events have happened at the same time, people moving to the city, people returning to it, people starting presses and reading series, so that over the last six or so years a confluence of poetic energy has occurred in Chicago. School or no school, some major literary happening has occurred in Chicago, and we hope that we have captured some of its vitality, some of its distinctly Midwestern essence in this collection.

William Allegrezza

Acknowledgements

First, we would like to thank Simone Muench for the wonderful title of this book.

Second, we would like to thank the many wonderful writers who made this project successful, and we would like to extend our special gratitude to Paul Hoover for his help. We would also like to thank Waltraud Haas and Lori Ryan for emotional support.

Third, some of the poems first appeared in other journals or books. We would like to thank the following presses and journals for letting us reprint the work:
> Mayapple Press, *Fence, Moria, The Canary, Seven Corners, Quarter After Eight*, Tougher Disguises Press, *Dusie, Otoliths, Mirage #4/Period(ical)*, *Carve, Denver Quarterly*, O Books, University of Iowa Press, University of California Press, Litmus Press, Tougher Disguises Press, *Chicago Review, Near South Magazine*, Chicago Poetry Project Press, Flood Editions, *Tin Lustre Mobile, ACM Another Chicago Magazine*, University of Michigan Press, *Sentence Magazine*, Writers Garret of Dallas, Chicago Poetry Project Press.

Current and Forthcoming Books by Cracked Slab Books

Edging, Michelle Noteboom.
The City Visible: Chicago Poetry for the New Century, Eds.
     Raymond Bianchi and William Allegrezza.
Levitations, Garin Cycholl.
Holograms/Ologrammi, Marcello Frixione. Trans. Joshua Adams and
     Joel Calahan.

Cracked Slab Books was started to provide an outlet for experimental poetry and mixed media works. With the aim of publishing at least two books a year, Cracked Slab Books is dedicated to promoting new American writers and to introducing the English-speaking world to interesting international poetry and mixed media work.

Editor: William Allegrezza
Publisher: Raymond Bianchi

For more information, please visit our web site:
http://www.crackedslabbooks.com

Cracked Slab Books
PO Box 378608
Chicago, IL 60637
USA